UNDER THE CLOCK

UNDER THE CLOCK

THE STORY OF

Miller & Rhoads

EARLE DUNFORD &
GEORGE BRYSON

Published by The History Press
Charleston, SC 29403
www.historypress.net

Cover design by Natasha Momberger.

All images courtesy Valentine Richmond History Center unless otherwise noted.

First published 2008

Manufactured in the United States

ISBN 978.1.59629.529.2

Library of Congress Cataloging-in-Publication Data

Bryson, George T.
Under the clock : the story of Miller & Rhoads / George T. Bryson and Earle Dunford.
p. cm.
ISBN 978-1-59629-529-2
1. Miller & Rhoads. 2. Department stores--Virginia--Richmond--History. 3. Department store Santas--Virginia--Richmond. I. Dunford, Earle. II. Title.
HF5465.U64M553 2008
381'.14109755451--dc22

2008033421

To John W. West III,
whose devotion to his grandfather and love of Miller & Rhoads
helped make this book possible.

Contents

Acknowledgements

The authors are indebted to many people for this work about Miller & Rhoads. Among them are Bill Martin, Laura All, Meg Hughes, Beth Petty, Meg Eastman, Howell Perkins, Kathleen Albers, Carolyn Moffatt, John West, Milton Burke, Anne Denny, Jane Galleher, Emma Brown, Frances Jones, Amanda Tompkins, Frances Verschuure, Dave Suskind, Betty Dementi, Alson Knapp, Bob Hardy, Dorman Hartley, Mike Laing, Curt Reichstetter, Jody Weaver and dozens of others who contributed anecdotes, recollections and suggestions. Extra thanks go to our patient and supportive wives, Bette Hawkins Dunford and Carol Hudgens Bryson.

Any errors, of course, should be blamed not on those who aided the authors but on the authors themselves.

CHAPTER I

AN OVERVIEW

Early in the morning, the chartered bus full of elegant women would leave North Carolina. When they arrived in Richmond, a department store executive would greet them and present each of them with a rose. They would shop for several hours and leave their purchases at a will-call desk. Around 4:00 p.m., a porter would take their packages back to the bus, where an executive would wish them goodbye and ask them to hurry back.[1]

Miller & Rhoads did not consider the carriage trade its only customer base, but did cater to it in what merchandise the store sold and the way it sold it. There were always experienced retailers in management, but some key people seemed to have been chosen more for their social prestige. Nevertheless, the philosophy on the back of sales tickets stressed, "The most important things in a store are confidence in the integrity of the men who manage it, and the merchandise offered to its patrons. Between the patrons and the management there is more to be desired than mere selling, an abiding friendship is valued far above profit." Customer loyalty was always a keynote.

Sometimes patrons involved management without knowing it. One new employee was trying to wrap a package in velvet so there were no wrinkles for a stately customer who wore a celluloid collar and a bow tie. She tried cutting the twine with broken scissors; the customer asked if that was the best pair she had. She said yes, but she would have thought a store as large as Miller & Rhoads could do better. The customer left without comment but the next day brought the employee a pair of new scissors. He was Webster Rhoads Sr., president of the company.[2]

Miller & Rhoads, which called itself "the Shopping Center" before the advent of regional malls, had the first elevator of any retail establishment in Richmond and installed escalators earlier than most stores. When it was almost unheard of in the late nineteenth century, it had "one price for all" on its merchandise and clearly marked it. The store also claimed to be the first in Richmond to install electric lighting, the first in the area to use air freight and the first in the nation "to be completely air-conditioned" and to "revolutionize window display."[3]

For more than one hundred years, the company thought it was giving its customers that little extra attention they wanted—and, generally, it did. Its Santa Claus was so well-known that he was featured in the *Saturday Evening Post*. Its Book and Author Dinner—with Edward Weeks, editor of the *Atlantic Monthly*, as master of ceremonies—drew nationally acclaimed writers. Its Tea Room had strikingly beautiful models who chatted with women at lunchtime. The store's first-floor clock was a Richmond icon. When someone said, "I'll meet you under the clock," it was understood it was the Miller & Rhoads clock.

Gene Sarazen once drove golf balls in the store's sporting goods shop. Roberta Peters sang and Peter Nero played piano at the 100th anniversary celebration. For more than forty years, Sara Sue Sherrill (later Baker and still later Waldbauer) designed hats for women. "If they didn't have Sara Sue hats, they'd go in mourning," said one retired employee.[4]

Yet, after seventy-five years, Miller & Rhoads, beginning in the 1960s, started to suffer. Suburban shopping centers sprung up. The casually dressed, hurried shopper replaced the stylishly dressed, leisurely shopper. Downtown retail sales sagged. Branches, sometimes too small, were opened—sometimes too late. There was a friendly merger and then two hostile takeovers. In its last twelve years, the store had four presidents—just one fewer than in its previous ninety-three years. It capsized in 1990.

The closing of Miller & Rhoads was just one example of a city losing its premier department store. Within a few years the story was the same with Strawbridges in Philadelphia, Woodward & Lothrop in Washington, Filene's in Boston and Marshall Field in Chicago.

Sixteen years after its demise, its place in Richmond's history was assured when the Library of Virginia devoted an entire week "to commemorate the magic of a bygone Virginia tradition," with lectures and exhibits of Miller & Rhoads photographs and memorabilia.

At its closing, the company had roughly $120 million in sales and twenty-two outlets in Virginia and North Carolina—a considerable spurt from a century earlier.

CHAPTER 2

IN THE BEGINNING

In 1885, three Pennsylvanians—Linton O. Miller, Webster S. Rhoads and Simon W. Gerhart—with combined capital of $3,000 decided to leave their store in Reading and start a new operation in the South. On Saturday morning, October 17, Miller, Rhoads & Gerhart opened a twenty-two-foot by seventy-five-foot store at 117 East Broad Street. The staff of ten had made sure everything would be ready by the opening of the state fair the following Monday.[5] That was the year Richmond claimed the nation's first streetcar system.

Business was good enough in the first year to permit a modest expansion into a 22- by 110-foot store. Richmonders responded and the store moved in the fall of 1888 to 509 East Broad Street. This new building contained three floors and a basement. A national publication described the store as "dealing in dry goods, notions and fancy goods...and with a pretty fair trade throughout all this part of the country...They use the top floors of [the building] for the display of cloaks, shawls, jerseys, muslin underwear, etc., and the others for the sale of the general stock they carry. They employ about thirty-five persons in their sales departments."[6] Two years later, Gerhart left the partnership and the name contracted to Miller & Rhoads.

By that time, business was humming along so well that Rhoads tried to persuade an old friend, William Grant Swartz, to come south and superintend the operations of the first floor. "I have filled this position here along with my other duties," he wrote, "but I find my office work will not admit of my being on the floor as much as I would like to be." When Swartz hesitated, Rhoads wrote a second letter six days later, offering a salary of $1,000 a year—to go along with his previous promise: If he wished to go home, he would be offered the chance to do so twice a year for seven to ten days. In addition, Rhoads noted, he and Miller had been boarding for $20 a month and Gerhart paid only $25 a month "at one of the most fashionable boarding houses in the city."

Swartz declined the offer but did enter a partnership to open a store in Norfolk known as Miller & Rhoads and Swartz, which continued until 1927, when Swartz took over the whole business. (Miller & Rhoads bought it back in 1965.)

Meanwhile, back in Richmond, business flourished and expansion continued. In 1917, the year Miller died, the store expanded onto Grace Street, with a structure of five stories and a basement. Some old-timers found it hard to accept the replacement of residences by a commercial venture. Margaret McGuire Gordon recalled, "It was a little dry goods

The elegance of 1885.

After three years, a happy retail family.

Retail stretch of Broad Street, about 1900.

THE EVENING LEADER—MANCHESTER AND RICHMOND, VA., FRIDAY, MAY 6, 1898.

Miller & Rhoads

PRICES TAKE A TUMBLE;
ALL FORMER BARGAIN-GIVING DISCOUNTED!

Our Small-Profit Selling Changed to a Sale Below Cost!

TO-MORROW "WE LAY OURSELVES OUT," TO REDUCE OUR STOCK OF

Silks, Dress Goods,
Tailor-Made Suits,
Separate Skirts,
Silk Shirt Waists.

We have the biggest and best stock we've ever owned, and the prices are right; but quantities demand an immediate reduction, and these stocks

MUST SUCCUMB TO CUT PRICES.

Do not miss your chance to secure great bargains.

Cut-Price Sale of Black and Colored Silks.

Black Brocaded India Silks, 22 inches wide in large and medium designs; our regular [illegible] goods—cut price [illegible] per yard.
Black Brocaded Grenadines 22 inches wide, in large designs, and very cheap at [illegible]—cut price [illegible] per yard.
Black [illegible] Brocades, 19 inches wide in small, medium and large effects; our regular [illegible] and [illegible] values—cut price [illegible] per yard.
Six pieces striped Taffetas, all pure Silk and extra wide, regular $1.00 values—cut price [illegible] per yard.
Checked Louisines with small Jacquard Figures; regular $1.00 values—cut price [illegible] per yard.
Five pieces Checked Taffetas, 19 inches wide, all pure Silk; were cheap at [illegible]—cut price [illegible] per yard.
Six pieces Foulard Silks, 27 inches wide, in large designs; regular [illegible] and [illegible] values—cut price [illegible].
Four pieces Checked Japanese Taffetas, 21 inches wide; regular price 42c.—cut price [illegible].
Two pieces Plaid Satins, 19 inches in bright colorings; regular price [illegible]—cut price [illegible].

Cut-Price Sale of Colored Dress Goods.

Four pieces Printed Indias, 30 inches wide, Dark Grounds with small figures; regular 25c. goods—cut price 12 1-2c. per yard.
Seven pieces Novelty Checks and Mixtures, All-Wool, and Wool and Raw Silk mixed, good values at [illegible] and 29c.—cut price [illegible] per yard.
Eight pieces Novelty Mixtures, 38 inches wide, regular [illegible] values—cut price [illegible] per yard.
Four pieces Silk and Wool Checks 38 inches wide; original price 50c.—cut price [illegible] per yard.
Six pieces of Illuminated Checks, 35 inches wide; original price [illegible]—cut price [illegible] per yard.
Five pieces Diagonal Suitings, 42 inches wide, all pure Wool and our regular [illegible] goods—cut price [illegible].

Cut-Price Sale Of Black Dress Goods.

Black Pebble Suitings, 38-inches wide, original price, 25c.; cut price, 12 1-2c. per yard.
Black Figured Mohairs, 38-inches wide, regular price, 39c.; cut price, [illegible] per yard.
Black Granite Cloth, light weight, 38-inches wide and all pure wool, regular price, 50c.; cut price, 42c.
Black Wool Grenadine, 42-inches wide and all pure wool, regular price, [illegible]; cut price, [illegible].
Black Striped Etamine, 42-inches wide, regular $1.00 value; cut price, [illegible].
Bayadere Stripe, 42-inches wide, all-wool and silk mixed, regular price, [illegible]; cut price, $1.25.
Black Figured Mohairs, 40-inches wide, regular $1.50 goods; cut price, $1.00 per yard.
Black Cheviot, All-Wool, 40 inches wide, original price, 59c.—cut price, [illegible].

Our Great Cut-Price Sale of Tailor-Made Suits, Skirts, and Silk Waists.

Here go the finest Suits of the season for the price of a cheap suit. We have reasons for selling these Suits at a loss, and sell we must—and quickly. Every Garment is made to fit perfectly.

TAILOR-MADE SUITS—Were $22.50, now [illegible]; in plain cloth, pompadour serge, and cheviot serges, jacket silk lined, strap seams.
SUITS—Were $14.50, now $10.50; in black and navy cheviot serge, reefer and tight-fitting jacket.
SUITS—Were $15.00 and $20.00, now [illegible]; reefer fly front and tight-fitting jackets, nicely made and finished.
SUITS—Were $17.50, now [illegible]; in tan covert cloth, tight-fitting, strap seams, jacket silk lined.
SUITS—were $10.50, now $8.49; reefer jacket, in green, brown, tan and navy serge.
SUITS—Were $15.00, now $12.50; in navy serge, reefer fly front jacket, perfect fit.

A Great Shirt-Waist Sale.

Your Pick of 1,500 Shirt Waists, on our Second Floor. Indeed this department is in full swing, and represents a harvest of economical SHIRT-WAIST BARGAINS, and you are bid to come—and get your share of this cutting.

Your pick of [illegible] Waists, were 50c. now [illegible], detached collar, all sizes.
Your pick of [illegible] Waists, were $1.00, now 75c. in Plaids, Plain Black and White Lawn.
Your pick of [illegible] Waists, were [illegible] now 98c. in fancy Checks, Plaids, Stripes, Plain Black and White Lawn.
Your pick of [illegible] Waists, were 75c. now 50c. in large variety of Plaids, Checks and Stripes.

Silk Waists.

SILK WAISTS—Were [illegible] and [illegible], now [illegible]; green and white plaid taffeta, deep single point yoke, very stylish.
SILK WAISTS—Were [illegible], now [illegible]; full blouse front, all shades, nicely made.
SILK WAISTS—Were [illegible], now [illegible]; elegant designs, excellent quality, perfect fit.
SILK WAISTS—Were [illegible], now $5.98; in light and dark Scotch plaid, and Roman stripe.

Wash Goods Sale.

10,000 Yards of New Wash Stuffs for the Hot Season.

SCOTCH CHEVIOTS, MADRAS,
MADRASSINE, LAWN,
ORGANDIE, FINE GINGHAMS,
BATISTE, MULLS,
LAPPETS, BROKEN PLAIDS,
AND BROKEN PRICES.

Cut Prices on Umbrellas.

UMBRELLAS—Were $1.00, now [illegible]; ladies' and gents' twill gloria, natural handles.
UMBRELLAS—Were $1.25, now 98c.; ladies' and gents' 26-inch silk-warp gloria.
UMBRELLAS—Were $1.50, now $1.25; ladies' and gents' 26-inch taffeta, case and tassle.
UMBRELLAS—Were $2.00, now [illegible]; ladies' and gents' 26-inch taffeta, silver swedge, natural handles.
UMBRELLAS—Were $2.00, now $1.69; gents' 28-inch taffeta, paragon frame, congo handles.

Cut Prices On Muslin Underwear.

LADIES' GOWNS—Were $1.75, $2.00 and $2.25, now [illegible]; made of cambric and cotton, cut full.
GOWNS—Were 59c., now 39c.; pleated yoke, cambric ruffle, cut full length.
CORSET COVERS—Were 12c., now 7 1-2c. each; plain, high and low neck.
CORSET COVERS—Were 19c., now 12 1-2c. each; low neck, lace trimmed.
DRAWERS—Were 25c., now 15c. pair; made of standard cotton, plain finished off with tucks.
DRAWERS—Were 39c., now 27c. pair; wide umbrella, deep cambric ruffle.
SKIRTS—Were 39c., now 27c.; made of standard cotton, with deep ruffle.
UMBRELLA SKIRTS—Were 69c., now 39c.; finished off with deep ruffle of cambric.
CHEMISES—Were 35c., now 25c.; cut full length, finished off with ruffle of cambric.
INFANTS' SLIPS—Were 25c., now 15c.; made of fine cambric, ruffle of cambric around neck and sleeves.
CHILD'S DRAWERS—Were 12 1-2c. and 15c., now 9c.; made of good, heavy cotton, finished off with tucks and deep hem.

Dress Trimmings.

A Sale! A Sale! 5,000 yards of Gimps and Braids at 2c., 5c., 6c., 10c. This represents about one-half value. The best stock of Trimmings in town, and at our popular low prices.

Cut-Price Sale Chinaware, Lamps, &c.

Reducing an enormous stock! Cutting prices right and left. This is your chance for bargains. Do you need a Dinner Set, Tea Set, Lamps, or Glassware? Do you contemplate arranging for summer boarders? If so, here's your chance to buy cheap.

Miller & Rhoads, **"The Always-Busy Store."**

Forerunner of discount ads, 1898.

The Times Dispatch

INDUSTRIAL SECTION

RICHMOND, VA., SUNDAY, FEBRUARY 1, 1914. PRICE FIVE CENTS.

THE MILLER & RHOADS GREAT DEPARTMENT HOUSE

GREATNESS FROM SMALL BEGINNING

Miller & Rhoads's Big Store Shows How the Thing Is Done.

PUSHING MEN AND RICHMOND HUSTLE

Square Dealing and Hard Work Build Up Establishment That All Virginia Is Proud Of. Quarter of Century Growth Described, and Reasons for It.

TOWN OF ALBERTA, AT THE CROSSING

New Tobacco Market and Manufacturing Town.

HOTEL, BANK AND SCHOOL NOW BUILT

Woodworking Plants Started. Many Fine Homes—Union Depot, Wholesale House and Retail Stores—Freight Rates Low as the Lowest—Tobacco Warehouses.

SHOULD EDUCATE FOR LIFE ON FARM

Suggestions of Man Who Looks to Agriculture to Save the Country.

PRACTICE THAT BEATS THEORY

Use of Hoe and Plow May Be Taught in Public Schools.

DEMONSTRATION IS DEMONSTRATED

District and County Agents Assembled at Blacksburg for Conference and Work.

POLYTECHNIC INSTITUTE AIDS

Review of Good Work Being Done and Yet to Be Done.

Expansion merits page-one coverage, 1914.

Linton O. Miller, founder. *Courtesy* Richmond Times-Dispatch.

store on Broad Street" when, from 1885 to 1905, she was growing up at 513 East Grace Street, the site of what was to become Berry-Burk & Co.[7] As early as 1919, Miller & Rhoads had five representatives in the *New York Times*'s list of buyers in the city.

In 1924, major expansion of Miller & Rhoads occurred on Grace Street from Sixth Street to Fifth. With five floors, the store boasted brand-new sales areas considered to be the latest style. Many were inspired by B. Altman in New York. In addition, motorized delivery service began, and a bank of ten elevators was installed. By the store's fiftieth anniversary in 1935, it had almost a million square feet of floor space and entrances on Broad, Grace, Fifth and Sixth Streets.

Of the three founders of the store, Rhoads was the dominant personality. His son, Webster Jr., said, "My father's conservatism was balanced by the more aggressive merchandising policies of his partner [Miller]."[8] Yet it was Rhoads Sr. whom old Richmonders tended to remember. Douglas Southall Freeman editorialized in the *Richmond News Leader* that Rhoads had "a master plan for his life, for his philanthropies and for his business...he rarely had trouble in determining promptly whether a new detail fitted into the broad plan."[9] Gerhart was rarely mentioned by the store as it moved through the twentieth century. In 1960, when Rhoads Jr. recounted in a speech the store's seventy-five years, he didn't refer to Gerhart at all. Indeed, Rhoads talked of "the two Northern gentlemen who set up shop in an old city."[10] That same year, the store's public

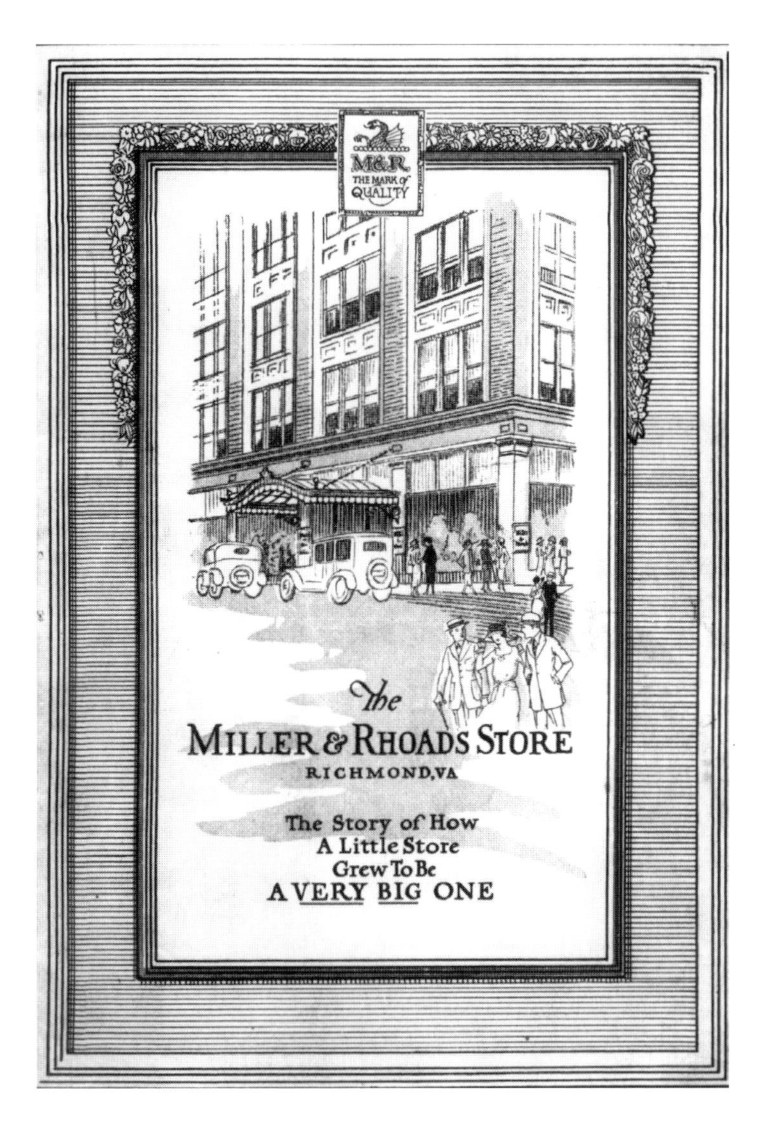

M&R's first store on Grace Street, 1917.

relations director tried to persuade the business editor of the *Richmond Times-Dispatch* not to mention Gerhart in a story on M&R's anniversary. He failed.

The employer-employee relationship at Miller & Rhoads may have been pleasant, but there was no air of permissiveness. Judy Bolling, who worked in the purchasing department, recalled that her mother, an employee before her, said that Linton O. Miller greeted employees at the entrance each morning. If one was late, he was sent to the balcony and told to sit for an hour.[11] His next paycheck was then docked an hour. Rhoads kept tabs on even routine operations of the store. One day he walked through the basement before going home to lunch. At a table where rayon underwear was on sale he picked up a handful, let it run through his fingers and commented, "You might as well be selling spaghetti."[12]

In the corporate world, there is nothing unique about management's claim that its employees are "like a family." But Miller & Rhoads executives—and many people far

Accessories Department, first floor, 1924.

The complete department store, 1924.

A well-staffed Cosmetics Department.

By 1924, the store had a full bank of elevators.

down the power ladder—seemed truly to believe it. In the early 1900s, there was a Twenty-Year Club, with an annual banquet, which continued until the store closed. By 1910, there was a company publication, entitled *Miller & Rhoads Monthly Record*. By 1942, it was the *MirroR*. There was even a theme song—a play on Cole Porter's "You're the Top"—printed in the newsletter that year.

In the early 1920s, Miller & Rhoads was offering a broad array of services to customers. In the basement were a lost-and-found desk and a free parcel checking desk. Public telephones were available on each floor. On the first floor were a list of theaters, local bank checks, schedules of trains and buses, a stamp and telegraph service and an "information bureau." All those services in later years were handled by the "lady under the clock."

In its early years, Miller & Rhoads was looking out for its employees. Its top three executives (Miller, Rhoads and A.B. Laughon, secretary and general manager) signed a letter in 1911 thanking Miss Lottie Scher for "your good service to us" and enclosed some material for a tablecloth on the occasion of her coming marriage. (Despite her four years with the company, the officers managed to misspell her name.)

The same month, the *Miller & Rhoads Monthly Record* reported: "Miss Lottie Scher (now Mrs. Sam Schuchat) entertained informally a few of her business associates at her residence, 1212 E. Broad Street. Miss Eleanor Finch and Louise Witte entertained the company with several selections of music which enlivened the party. Then Miss Ethel DuVal, who is noted for her wit and humor, gave us a recitation on 'Aunt Isabella's Courtship.'"[13]

The M&R family came in two colors, black and white, and essentially it was two families. Whites in the Twenty-Year Club held their annual get-togethers in the Tea Room; blacks in the basement of the Mosque (now the Landmark Theater). Activities of black employees were dutifully chronicled in the *MirroR*, but under a separate heading, "Colored Employees." Miller & Rhoads, of course, was itself mirroring the separate-but-equal policy in effect at all levels of the South into the 1960s.

Miller & Rhoads did succeed in convincing customers that it was special. That may have grown out of the policy of reimbursing customers for merchandise they deemed unsatisfactory. The younger Rhoads said his father and Miller "adhered to a policy of exchanging, or giving credit for, any article bought in the store. Unless the customer was obviously trying to take advantage of them, these exchanges were always made without question. As the store and its personnel grew, the partners had desks side by side in a small office, but they continued to sell personally and to remain available to any customer who wanted to exchange merchandise."[14]

Rhoads recalled one female customer whose exchanges caused the buyer of the department to double as private detective. He said,

> *Every year she would come in and charge to her account an opera cape; and every year, a few days later, she would return it. One year as she "bought" an extremely handsome cape, the buyer of the department observed that the opera was coming to Richmond. He bought a ticket himself and during the intermission searched through the lobby until he found this lady—beautiful in her Miller & Rhoads cape. With the greatest friendliness he went up, addressed himself to her, and complimented her on how lovely she looked in the cape. The cape was not returned.*[15]

CHAPTER 3
FIFTIETH ANNIVERSARY

The beginning of Miller & Rhoads's fiftieth anniversary celebration occurred February 18, 1935, when, as described in the in-house publication, a "golden chariot" was pulled through the store. It was designed by Addison Lewis and other staff decorators and contained John and Phillip West, grandsons of Webster Rhoads Sr. John was presented a "golden key" and, like any normal eight-year-old, tried repeatedly and unsuccessfully to stick it in the lock to the Fifth Street entrance before a helpful soul said, "Pretend."

That was John West's unofficial start with M&R. The official start was in 1957, when, after five years with B. Altman & Co., he joined M&R's new store in Roanoke. In the ensuing years he became manager of the downtown store in Charlottesville and three stores in Richmond—Southside Plaza, Chesterfield Town Center and Regency Square—before retiring in 1982. He is a walking encyclopedia of Miller & Rhoads.

For M&R's fiftieth anniversary, an anonymous member of the store's Twenty-Year Club penned a four-paragraph tribute, "My Store," in which he proclaimed, "I believe in you for the noble institution you are; a thing of life pulsating with energy and animated with the sole purpose to serve."

The store printed a booklet celebrating "Fifty Years of Progressive Merchandising" and containing pictures of each floor, space for autographs of employees and a description in purple prose of each floor. The street floor contained a linen department, where "brides-to-be assemble entire trousseaux, no matter how simple or magnificent...and brides of yesteryear replenish stocks." On the second floor, the Walnut Room "is an exclusive shop where a distinguished clientele receives personalized, individual attention...where the latest ideas of fashion are translated into exquisite materials and executed with those satisfying standards of workmanship which give them the stamp of perfection."

Even in the basement, "quality is not sacrificed to price. All merchandise here, as elsewhere, is perfect quality." At that same level, "A pleasant hour can be spent anytime in the radio shop...with good music, or exciting police radio calls, or foreign broadcasts." In another section of the basement was the Boys' Own Shop, where "young gentlemen find the smart, tweed-y casual clothes they like so well."

As part of its golden jubilee, Miller & Rhoads picked a "Miss 1885." She was Betty Collins, whose mother, Carolyn, began working at the store when a student at John Marshall High School and rose to buyer for infants and teens. Betty's grandmother, who

John and Phillip West, the founder's grandsons, at the fiftieth anniversary. *John West Private Collection.*

was a seamstress in 1885, the year of the store's founding, made her granddaughter a costume dating back to that era. It still hangs in the closet of Betty Collins Walker.[16]

There was an air of refinement throughout the store. Erna Darg came to Richmond from London, where she had worked at "the rather posh Oxford Street department store, Selfridge's." Her son Peter recalled that the people in the personnel department at M&R thought her British accent was perfect for someone in the hosiery department, where she worked in the late '50s and early '60s. The store even hired another Britisher, Amy Jordan, to work in the department. Peter Darg says stockings were kept in flat, rectangular boxes and each pair was wrapped in neatly folded tissue. Most came from North Carolina mills, but there also were Schapiarelli at seven dollars a pair. "The hosiery counter," he said, "was quite long (and not far from the clock) and usually had about half a dozen sales assistants who spent all day discussing color shades and caressing the merchandise for customers."[17]

Charlotte Moss, who grew up in Richmond, is one of the nation's foremost decorators. In *House Beautiful* magazine, she says that her grandmother worked in the china department of Miller & Rhoads, and "that's where I got my china gene."[18]

About the time of its fiftieth anniversary, Miller & Rhoads came out with a small, twenty-eight-page booklet titled *Market Places*, setting the scenes in Richmond and the

Webster S. Rhoads, Jr., Chairman of the Board, addressed store employees at opening of the Seventy-Fifth Anniversary yeaı

In opening this meeting that inaugurates Miller & Rhoads' Diamond Jubilee Year it is my first desire to thank you, the members of the Miller & Rhoads store family, for your many contributions to Miller & Rhoads and to pay tribute to all of your predecessors over the seventy-five years for their contribution to Miller & Rhoads. I am sure that my father and Mr. Linton O. Miller would express these same sentiments to you were they here today.

(Continued on Page 4)

Portrait of the late Mr. Webster S. Rhoads, Sr.

Webster Rhoads Sr. and successor Webster Rhoads Jr.

Mideast. Two thousand years ago, in Baghdad, the booklet started, there were "dusky Algerians...copper-hued Nubians...Moorish Masters...Bearded Jews. For it was bazaar day and the Gods of Commerce looked with amusement on this, the first department store."

From there, the reader was taken through all the floors of Miller & Rhoads, each with its distinctive sections, until he reached "Evening in Baghdad," where "the sun in a last vain effort tints the market square with fading purples and dim golds."

Then to "Evening in Richmond":

> *Five-thirty p.m.—The last stray shopper has left the alluring bargain, the cash registers have emitted their final clang, and the employees, tired, but filled with the joy of work well done, of one more day added to the list of things worth while, file out the massive doors and wend their homeward way.*
>
> *Weary executives have left their desks, tired trucks have rumbled home, the frantic elevators are stilled, the eager sales-people are departed, the busy bus boys are gone, for Miller & Rhoads have hewn another day of promise from the future and added it to those of achievement of the past.*

The vision that Webster S. Rhoads had in 1885 had become a reality. He continued in the presidency until ill health forced him to give it up to his son in 1940. When the elder Rhoads died the following year, the employee newsletter said he was "a man who was never too busy to stop his own work to listen to others' problems, no matter how small or insignificant, and to suggest what often proved to be the happy solution; never too concerned with his own affairs to lend a helping hand or give a cheering smile."

CHAPTER 4
WORLD WAR II

The store added its sixth, seventh and eighth floors in 1941, months before the United States entered World War II. By May 1942, Webster Rhoads Jr., who had been president only since 1940, joined the Army Air Corps as a second lieutenant. Absalom B. Laughon, who had been with M&R since 1894 and its vice-president and general manager since 1917, ascended to the presidency. Until Rhoads returned to civilian life in early 1945, there was dual management with Laughon and F.T. Bates Jr., treasurer.

During the war, the store dripped patriotism. Its display windows featured such things as a salute to women in service. On June 6, 1944, when Allied forces invaded Europe, Miller & Rhoads set up "Liberation Day" windows, featuring prayers from officers in the armed forces. Less than a year later, on May 8, 1945, when the European war ended, there were new "Prayer Windows," with photographs of servicemen and prayers from religious leaders in Richmond.

As men entered the armed forces, there were changes at the store. Women replaced men as elevator operators. Employees collected scrap metal. They also were encouraged by the in-house newsletter to buy their bonds and stamps through payroll deductions.

Early in the war, Miller & Rhoads transformed its premier window—the one at Sixth and Grace Streets—into a Victory Window elaborately decorated in red, white and blue, where war bonds and stamps were sold. Governor Colgate W. Darden Jr. bought the first stamp. An advertisement proclaimed, "We don't need to emphasize that War Stamps and Bonds are the best things we have to sell, and that is why the most important window in our store has been turned into an office for the duration. Every day volunteers from the office of Civilian Defense are on duty. Many are your friends and would like to see you." Many celebrities who were touring the country to promote war bonds visited the window, including Lon MacAllister, star of the movie *Winged Victory*.

War or no war, Richmonders still needed to shop, although some items were hard to come by, like hosiery for women. There was a "victory garden" on West Broad Street, far away from the store downtown. When the store had trouble getting enough chickens for the Tea Room, John Marchant went back to his native Middlesex County, visited farmers and brought chickens back to Miller & Rhoads.[19]

Em Bowles Locker Alsop said that Miller & Rhoads "was more like a family during the war than before or after." She should know, since her association there began with a

Left: Three floors added, 1941. *Courtesy* Richmond Times-Dispatch.

Below: Window shows that women were also patriotic.

Every little bit helps the war effort.

War bonds are promoted in the store's major window. *Courtesy Virginia Historical Society.*

Lon McAllister of *Winged Victory* fame didn't mind posing. *Courtesy Virginia Historical Society.*

fashion show in 1935 and, after years in New York, she was back with the store throughout the war writing copy in the advertising department.

Mrs. Alsop recalls shortages of shoes and of material for clothing. People were making their own garments, she said, and they bought the required fabrics at Miller & Rhoads, thus creating a rush on that department and the resulting shortage. With gasoline rationed, people reduced their downtown shopping trips. So they telephoned, and one woman in the linen department "took orders all day by phone."

Some routines didn't change. "Richmond ladies continued their patronage of Miller & Rhoads," she said. They met at the glove department on the first floor before going to the Tea Room.[20] For people fortunate enough to have more than the minimum gasoline ration, a trip to Miller & Rhoads was still important. One resident of Prince Edward County said he saw people he knew from all around the state when he made the trip to Richmond.

Major construction was almost impossible in the early '40s for anything unrelated to the war effort. But Miller & Rhoads announced it would build a twelve-story structure at Sixth and Broad Streets as soon as possible. The proposed amenities were eye-opening:

Miller & Rhoads shared space in the new Woolworth Building. *Courtesy* Richmond Times-Dispatch.

This version of the store was a "downtown" postcard. *Milton Burke Private Collection.*

a 1,500-seat auditorium, a new Tea Room, a men's restaurant with an "exposed kitchen charcoal grill in old-time Southern fireplace kitchen style" and a "Lilliput" dining room for children. Far ahead of the game, M&R said, "Television facilities are planned on an elaborate scale to link up windows, the auditorium and specified departmental events throughout the store." The realities of the postwar economy shelved that project. Instead the company vacated the Corner Shop, a former dime store at Fifth and Broad, and entered a deal with F.W. Woolworth.

Miller & Rhoads had owned all of the south side of Broad Street between Fifth and Sixth Streets except for the Woolworth building, second from the corner at Fifth. When a construction deal was worked out, a new Woolworth's store was erected. M&R occupied a portion of the new first and second floors and all of the fourth floor—an entire city block. Woolworth retained the third floor of the new building. This completed the expansion that had begun in 1885, and for forty years the store looked as it did at closing.

CHAPTER 5
COMPETITION ACROSS THE STREET

For all of its 105 years, Miller & Rhoads's chief competitor was Thalhimers, founded 43 years earlier and, for most of both stores' lives, right across Sixth Street from M&R. But the competition did not preclude cooperation. John Marchant, a retired M&R president, said the stores worked together—but never setting prices—on things such as charity drives. As early as the 1940s, they jointly ran a parking garage on nearby Grace Street. It had a capacity of one thousand cars. In the late 1940s, executives of both stores made an annual wager, paid off in bottles of Scotch whiskey to their counterparts across the street, on who compiled the better year economically, based on their annual reports.

Downtown shoppers routinely crossed Sixth Street in the middle of a block to go from one store to the other. That sounded like jaywalking, technically, and the stores certainly didn't want their customers to be ticketed as law breakers. So they sought help from the city's traffic engineer, John Hanna. Not wanting to play lawyer, Hanna sought an opinion from the city attorney, who ruled that because an alley ran behind Thalhimers, it was really an extension of a street; thus, walking across Sixth Street in the middle of that block was not really jaywalking.

There was also cooperation on more mundane matters. One former executive of M&R said that if the wife of one of its top officials wanted a particular item and the store was out of it, he would hustle across to Thalhimers to fetch it. Robert Hardy, an M&R vice-president, once nonchalantly strolled across Sixth Street with a gun in hand to exchange it for a weapon that Thalhimers had.

One customer, Louise Lipscomb, said that when the mother of a friend pulled a charge plate from her purse to pay for a Miller & Rhoads blouse, she found that what she had was, instead, a Thalhimers plate. Unfazed, the clerk opened an M&R account for her daughter.[21]

Webster Rhoads Jr. joined the company in 1929 and succeed his father as president in 1940. The year before his entering the Army Air Corps and the seven years before his becoming board chairman in 1953 meant he spent a total of eight years as president. He was tall, handsome and popular. John Marchant, a later president, described him as "a perfect gentleman," although "working was not really his long suit."[22] Rhoads sat on the corporate boards and served the nonprofit groups that one in his business and social position would be expected to do—such as the United Negro College Fund, the Virginia Museum of Fine Arts and Colonial Williamsburg.

William Taliaferro, Edwin Hyde, Alfred Thompson and Webster Rhoads Jr. gloat over Thalhimers annual financial statement. *Courtesy Virginia Historical Society.*

As president of the company, Rhoads inherited Elizabeth Pitts as his secretary. She had joined M&R as a teenager and became secretary to his father. Sumpter Priddy, longtime executive of the Virginia Retail Merchants Association, said, "She had a cranky voice and a cranky personality and knew where the bones were buried." Rhoads tried one day to get away from her and sought refuge in the accounts receivable office on the same floor. She stormed out and asked, "Has anyone seen that long-legged son of a bitch?"

Once spotted, Rhoads replied, "Elizabeth, are you looking for me?"[23]

Rhoads bought a plantation, Elmington in Gloucester County, and commuted from there to Richmond on Monday mornings and returned Thursday evenings. He kept an apartment at the Prestwould and later the Berkshire.[24] He was driving near Elmington when he suffered a heart attack and died just days after his fifty-ninth birthday in 1967. Governor Mills E. Godwin Jr. said, "His record of public service to the state and to his community has placed him in the high ranks of those who give voluntarily of themselves for the good of the common men."

Webster Rhoads Jr. was not the only son of a founder to achieve executive status with the company. Earl Miller, son of Linton O. Miller, became a vice-president, but apparently had few duties other than to be in charge of security. His office was on the

Shoppers routinely crossed the middle of the block on Sixth Street. *Courtesy* Richmond Times-Dispatch.

seventh floor, where other executives were housed, and he was used to going there immediately upon entering the store.

One day a young sales clerk stopped him as he surveyed the men's apparel on the first floor and told him to go back outside the Fifth Street entrance, whence he had come, and wait until 9:00 a.m., when the store opened for business. He did as was told, reentered the store and went up the escalator to the seventh floor. The young clerk was brought up short by an older salesman, who informed him that the man he'd sent outside was Vice-president Earl Miller. No hard feelings resulted.

At the Willow Lawn branch, the operations manager, Frederick A. Dill, was called to the general office, where a secretary told him to do something about "a little, old man" who would come to her desk and read the morning newspaper. Dill informed her that it was Earl Miller; they met and became friends, Dill said.[25]

After returning from service in World War II, William B. Thalhimer Jr. and Webster S. Rhoads Jr. became the chief executives of their respective stores. Thalhimers had been operated continuously by the same family that had started it in 1842. But Thalhimer and his brother Charles brought in some additional experienced retailers. Miller & Rhoads added its own stable of experienced executives: Alfred C. Thompson, vice-president and general manager; Raymond M. Munsch from Macy's as personnel and services vice-president; William P. Taliaferro as treasurer; and within its ranks, it promoted Gordon M. Mallonee and John R. Marchant.

Still, Miller & Rhoads was more tempting to the well-heeled customer, and some of its executives were more likely to be in what passed for the city's social register. Edwin

Hyde, who came to Miller & Rhoads in 1946 as a vice-president and moved up to the presidency, had been a banker. Thomas P. Bryan Jr., a lawyer and member of one of the city's most prestigious families, had been mayor before becoming a vice-president and secretary of the company. Penn Montague and William Ellyson Jr. were other executives with the proper social connections.

One M&R executive who definitely was not "old Richmond" or even "old Virginia" was Alfred C. Thompson, who joined the company in 1948 as general manager and rose to executive vice-president. Before Webster Rhoads Jr. hired him, Thompson had been with Associated Merchandising Corp., a buying group for stores that included Thalhimers. Even earlier he had been a boxer, sponsored by Wanamaker's, and had a cauliflower ear to show for it.

Thompson "never forgot he was from the wrong side of the tracks," said Sumpter Priddy, longtime executive of the Retail Merchants Association. Thompson would assemble salespeople and ask them what was going on in the real sales world "because we upstairs don't know." He bought a big house on Monument Avenue and gave Christmas and Easter parties for children and grandchildren of employees.[26] Always the merchandiser, Thompson wrote President Kennedy that he should start wearing a hat because men across the country were following the president's example, and hat sales had fallen precipitously.

Thompson had a slight speech impediment, and fellow executives snickered about his saying what sounded like "wolume is wital." He claimed it was painted in Latin on his living room ceiling.

CHAPTER 6

ALMOST ANYTHING YOU'D WANT

Miller & Rhoads, like other large stores, organized its departments based on such factors as physical location, buying and selling responsibility, personnel and other things related to efficiency. Its divisions were Fashions, Accessories, Home Furnishings, Menswear, Children's and Smallwears and Basement. The basement division duplicated some upstairs departments but operated as a separate entity with its own personnel.

Fashions received premier treatment in terms of space, decor, advertising and window and interior display. For example, the eleven large display windows on Grace Street were usually devoted to Fashions. Inside the store, almost the entire Grace Street side consisted of the Virginia Room for designer fashion, coats, suits, dresses, furs, bridals and lingerie.

To some people, the vision of the building was important. A North Carolina customer, wife of a clergyman, always wanted a room on the north wing of the Hotel John Marshall so she could open the curtains in the morning and see Miller & Rhoads.

Another visitor, Louise Lipscomb, recalled coming to Miller & Rhoads from Burkeville as a girl. It was "about the same as going to heaven," she said. Her family tried to get to the store twice a year—once before Christmas and once before Easter. Ms. Lipscomb wrote,

> *Whenever my sister or I needed new clothes, my mother took us to Mrs. Dance on the second floor in "Young Juniors." She was a remarkable woman who immediately recognized size changes, remembered color and style preferences, and tactfully observed the limits, that is, how much my mother would "put into" a dress or coat. Mrs. Dance served, too, as a mediator between Mother, who pictured something "sweet and girlish" in pink with sweetheart neckline, and my teenaged sister, who longed for something daring in black with sequins.*
>
> *As we girls grew older, we traveled across the second floor to the "Misses" department and became friends with Mrs. Thompson, who assumed Mrs. Dance's role of family counselor. These saleswomen never left a customer to fend for herself among the clothes racks. After learning from the customer what she wanted that day, the clerk would pick out a few things, then usher the customer into a fitting room and stay with her throughout the ordeal, helping take clothes off and put things on, buttoning, zipping, smoothing, rushing to find another size or a different color. Some women enjoyed the attention; those of us with holey underwear cringed.*

Sunday "Society" fashion advertisement.

"Style Marches On" in display window.

Everyone goes formal in this fashion window.

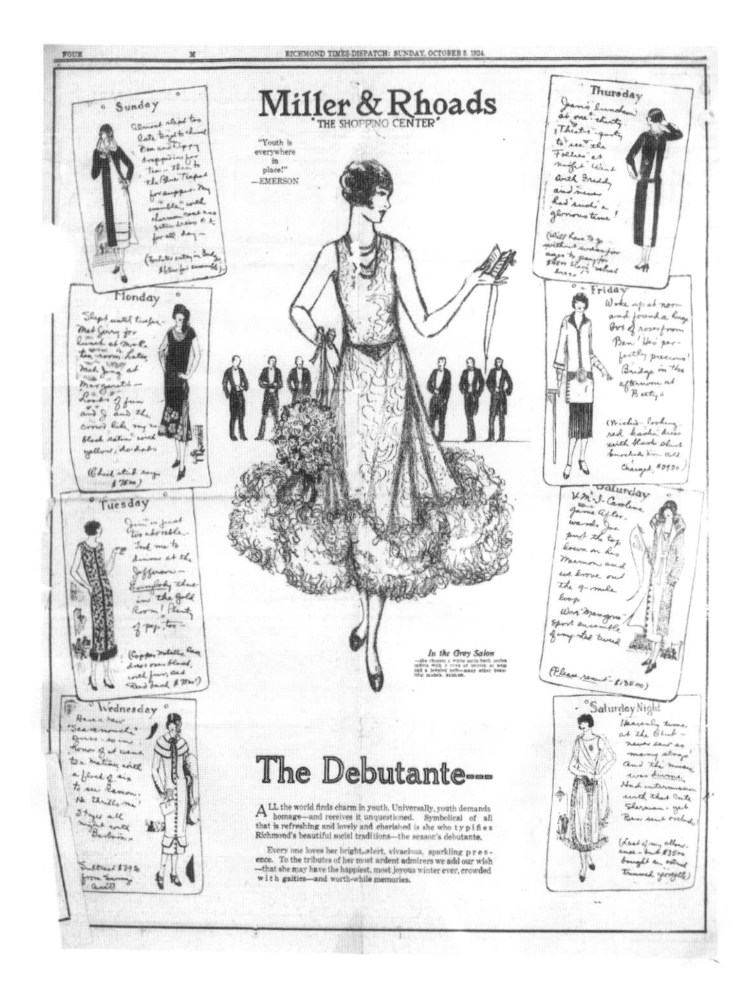

FOUR M RICHMOND TIMES-DISPATCH: SUNDAY, OCTOBER 5, 1924.

Miller & Rhoads

"THE SHOPPING CENTER"

"Youth is everywhere in place!" —EMERSON

The Debutante---

ALL the world finds charm in youth. Universally, youth demands homage—and receives it unquestioned. Symbolical of all that is refreshing and lovely and cherished is she who typifies Richmond's beautiful social traditions—the season's debutante.

Every one loves her bright, alert, vivacious, sparkling presence. To the tributes of her most ardent admirers we add our wish—that she may have the happiest, most joyous winter ever, crowded with gaities—and worth-while memories.

Above: This is the way it was done in 1911.

Left: How to look stylish in 1924.

Ms. Lipscomb said her mother made an appointment every two or three years with Sara Sue, Miller & Rhoads's hat designer, in the Amethyst Room. "A clerk would lead her into an inner room; then, a lady brought in unadorned hat forms big enough to fit Mother's head. Finally, Sara Sue herself would appear, mold the hat into some shape and place flowers, veils and ribbons on the brim, a ritual carried out with quiet, intense concentration."[27]

From a sales promotion standpoint, the most prestigious advertisement each week appeared in the Sunday "society" section of the *Times-Dispatch*. For many years, M&R advertised in national fashion magazines with designer merchandising and window tie-ins. Miller & Rhoads instituted a teen board and a college board to promote the proper fashions to their age groups.

At least some customers were convinced they were special. Nancy M. Phillips of Richmond recalled,

> *Back in the '40s as a teenager, going to Miller & Rhoads on Saturdays was the "in" thing to do. I think my mother knew someone by name in every department so that she could just call that person and order what she wanted.*

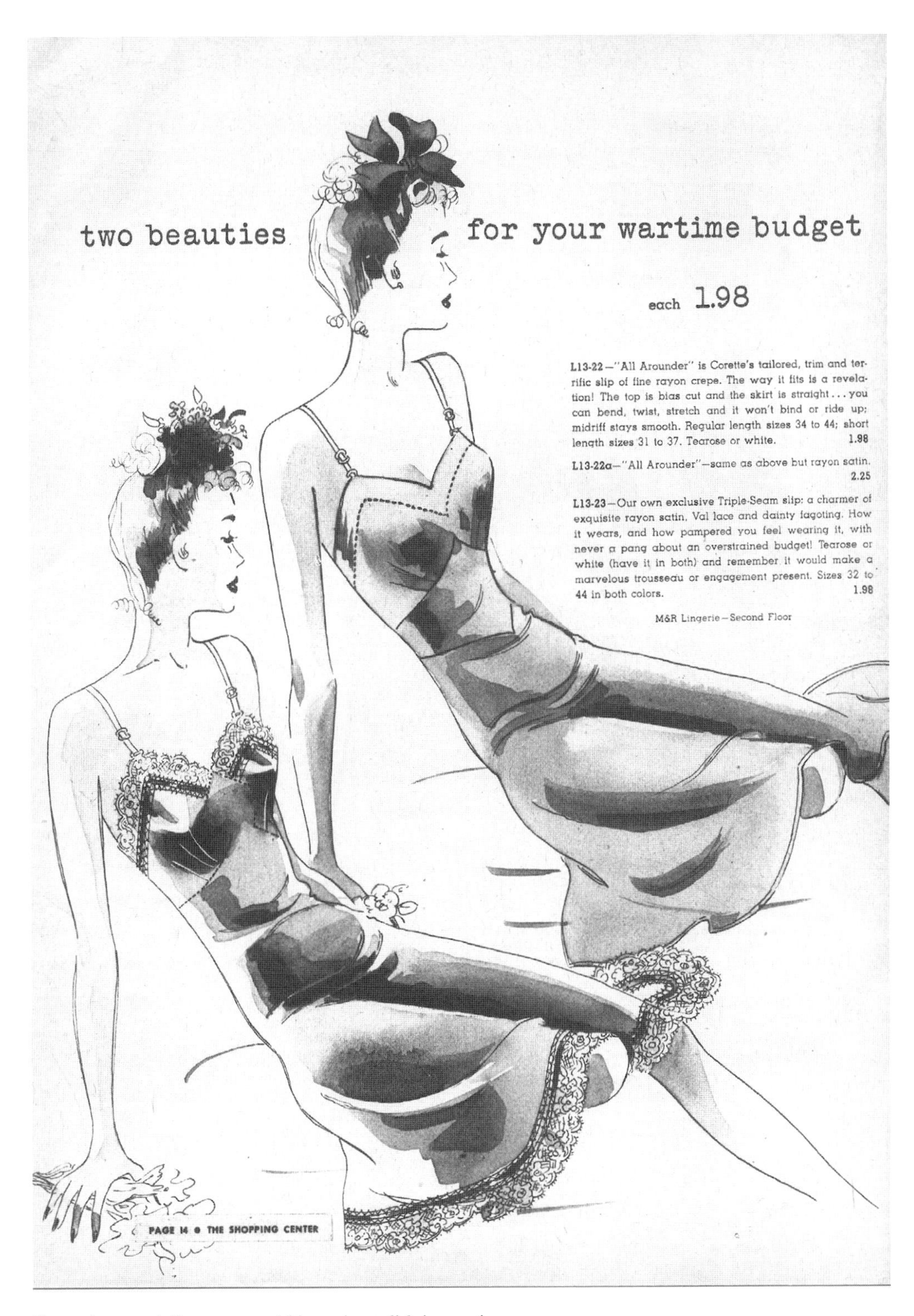

For under two dollars, you could be quite stylish in wartime.

The Amethyst Room was the ultimate in fashion.

> *I remember once being waved down by Miss Gibbs in the lingerie department, saying that my mother had called and asked her to be on the lookout for me and tell me I needed to call home. That personal touch meant a lot.*[28]

Another customer recalled that in the spring before her July wedding her mother was diagnosed with cancer "but determined to go through with my wedding."

> *When my mother was well enough, we would make the two-hour trip from my hometown to Miller & Rhoads. On the top floor of the store there was a medical center for the employees with a nurse. The manager of the store would let my mother go and rest on the bed they had there. Then I would run from floor to floor bringing her items that we needed to purchase for the wedding. From that bed, she directed how my veil should look, picked out her dress for the wedding and helped pick out the maid-of-honor dress. No one ever questioned my story every time I would ask to take items to the top floor.*

Tie-ins with fashion magazine.

They even brought her favorite meal (chicken pot pie) from the Tea Room…The bridal consultant even called the week after my wedding to see how my mother was feeling.[29]

In 1947, Mrs. Vernon Meredith Barnes of Wilson, North Carolina, received a note from the bridal coordinator at Miller & Rhoads. It said,

Just a year ago, it was our happy privilege to extend to you felicitations upon the occasion of your wedding.

To-day, we would like to remind you of our continued interest in your welfare and happiness, and our constant desire to be of service to you.[30]

The Accessories Division on the main floor was closely related to space and promotion of the Fashions Division . Thus, the sales staff was familiar to customers passing through on their way to other departments. Although shoes and better millinery were on the

Brides' Shop.

second floor, budget millinery and scarves were popular spots for sales promotion. Window promotions for accessories usually were on Sixth Street in view of the busy pedestrian traffic between M&R and Thalhimers.

Menswear was also on the first floor with a complete assortment of suits, sportswear, furnishings, hats (until the early 1960s) and boys' wear. One customer who came from Canada in 1939 at age ten with knickers recalls Mrs. Moran in the boys' department selling him his first pair of long trousers. A glance at the 1960 menswear catalogue shows that the width of neckties has changed, but the button-down shirt is still here after almost fifty years.

The Broad Street side of the second floor was the children's area. There the store offered the family every need from cradle to preteens to teens. The girls could hardly wait until their sizes and their mothers let them shop up on the third floor in the Junior Colony.

Miller & Rhoads adopted a "twin insurance" policy for expectant mothers. One customer who discovered in 1948 that she was to have two babies, not one, said, "Miller & Rhoads duplicated everything [I] had bought for the baby and delivered [the items]… in Emporia on a Miller & Rhoads truck."[31]

The Broad Street side of the third floor housed needlework, fabrics and assorted sewing needs characteristic of the store since its founding. One young girl, bored by her

Accessories department, main floor.

Menswear in the late '40s.

mother's dithering over goods in the fabric department, would pull strings from the ends of the multicolored fabric rolls, wrap them into a ball and drop them onto the elegant hats of the women descending the escalators. Was it worth it, someone asked? "Not often but it was worth the try," was the rejoinder.

Home Furnishings occupied an entire city block on the fourth floor. There were furniture, domestic and oriental rugs, linens and bedding. The interior design department

Left: Men's and women's shirts, circa 1960. *Dorman Hartley Private Collection.*

Below: "Wonderland of Toys" in window.

provided decor for many Richmond homes. Miss Hattie Jones was known to those with extensive budgets, although customers seeking more economical furnishings could go to the Home Advisory Service, where slightly less experienced decorators got their start. A former general manager of the downtown store said his two biggest headaches were created by "crooked draperies and late-delivery wedding dresses."

The fifth floor was something special. There was the glamorous Collectors' Corner for antiques, the huge china and crystal department, the wedding registry and services, plus the upscale gift shop next to the Tea Room. A woman who said she had sought antique candelabra unsuccessfully at the Silver Vaults in London found "just the thing" at the Collectors' Corner. Her husband gave them to her for Christmas.

One of the brides impressed by Miller & Rhoads's attention was Louise Dickson, who bought her wedding dress there in 1958. With the dress, in a small Miller & Rhoads box, was a coin to put in her shoe. With it was a poem: "Something borrowed, something blue, a lovely six-pence in her shoe."[32]

Up on the sixth floor was housewares and, for many years, appliances, toys and sporting goods. Webster Rhoads Jr. drew the line at creating a pet shop. Evidently, he felt that seasonal birds on the first floor would suffice.

Trying to please customers is standard advice from any store's management to its employees. At Miller & Rhoads, Grayson Collins took that seriously when working in the record department of the Corner Shop. One frequent customer liked listening to music in a soundproof booth, and she helped him with record choices. He was impressed by more than the music and later asked her to marry him. She became Mrs. Scott Carpenter.[33]

The Collectors' Corner, a unique department. *Courtesy* Richmond Times-Dispatch.

Spacious china department. *Courtesy Dementi Studios.*

Helen Taylor Heinzen, who worked in a variety of departments, had a difficult time satisfying one customer when she was handling sewing supplies. "One day," said Mrs. Heinzen, "a customer came to my counter and asked, 'Do you have a yard stick?' I showed her the yard stick and she said, 'Do you have one a little bit longer; this is so short.'"

Mrs. Heinzen began at M&R in the boys' department in 1949 but left soon to take a job "across the street." She went back to M&R after a few weeks, "begging to be rehired. I lost my seniority but [was] happy to be back," she said. Her stay at Miller & Rhoads until 1975 had another benefit. She married George Heinzen, who worked in the receiving department.[34]

Although the basement lacked the pizzazz of some upstairs departments, it was popular and usually crowded—with many who shopped upstairs, too. There also were the coffee shop, a shoe repair shop (quite busy during World War II because of a leather shortage), storage lockers and a will-call desk.

Two major bargain events caused frantic crowds. After waiting in line for the store opening, women rushed in for the "Sample Sale" and the "Down-from-Up Sale." The former could be enjoyed only by those fortunate enough to be able to wear a manufacturer's showroom sample size; but the latter was for everyone.

Waiting for the sale to begin.

Employees ham it up in a May Sale skit. *Jane Galleher Private Collection.*

Mrs. Woodrow Wilson is a Miller & Rhoads guest. *Courtesy* Richmond Times-Dispatch.

There were "white sales" in January and July, a home furnishings sale in February, warehouse sales in March and September, a May Sale (all departments) and a Harvest Sale in October, which also involved everything. One aspect of the May Sale enjoyed by the employees was the kickoff rallies in the Tea Room. Executives from Webster Rhoads Jr. and Edwin Hyde down to buyers participated in skits designed to spur the sales staff to greater heights.

One of the most popular and successful departments in the miscellaneous merchandise category was the Book Department on the first floor. Its position was unusual, since in most department stores that area was reserved for "high-traffic, high-profit" items. Perhaps the reason for its significant volume was Peggy O'Neill and her assistant, Emma Craddock, who once said that customers "would buy any title concerning Virginiana." Despite the wide range of fiction and nonfiction bestsellers, one of the hottest classifications was cookbooks. There was also a "Storybook Lady" who would read aloud to children. A feature of the department was visits from celebrities ranging from Mrs. Woodrow Wilson to Pearl Bailey. Miss Bailey was so popular that the store kept the department open past closing time so she could continue autographing books.

The luggage department was adjacent to books, although it moved extensively between floors six and three. One day a customer asked a sales clerk where she could find the luggage department. "If you'll stand here a minute," the clerk replied, "it's sure to go past."[35]

CHAPTER 7

YES, WE HAVE CELEBRITIES

Miller & Rhoads had its share of celebrity visitors—sometimes for a store function, other times for a collaborative venture. Frequently movie stars appearing at Loew's Theater across Sixth Street would drop by the Tea Room at lunchtime to be introduced.

Another was the case of Carol Channing, who was in town for the opening of the Carpenter Center nearby. Miss Channing was to have lunch at Miller & Rhoads. She was given directions from her hotel, walked a short distance to Sixth Street—and entered Thalhimers. There she got more directions, walked across the street to M&R and took an elevator to the Tea Room. The M&R executive, who was to have met her at the Fifth Street entrance, was almost apoplectic. Where was his guest? Finally he found his way to the Tea Room and met a quite calm Miss Channing, who proved to be as entertaining at lunch as she was on stage.

Erma Bombeck, the newspaper columnist, was another big hit in her appearance at Miller & Rhoads. The title of the book she was promoting was *Motherhood: The Second Oldest Profession*. One questioner wanted to know, "What is the world's oldest profession?"

"Agriculture," replied Miss Bombeck.

Gloria Vanderbilt was on hand one day to promote her line of blouses. The occasion was such a success that she said she had sold more blouses there than at any similar promotion in her company's history. That may have been the reason that she persuaded the store management to give her the secret recipe for the Tea Room's chocolate silk pie to take home to her sons, Wyatt and Anderson Cooper. The chef was told that Miss Vanderbilt lived in New York and certainly was not going to divulge the details to any M&R competitor. But, protested the chef, he made fifty pies at a time. Grudgingly, he broke down the recipe by figuring one-fiftieth of each ingredient.

Certain celebrities would appear only after a detailed contract was signed. Miller & Rhoads was happy to go along with stipulations for type of hotel room, menu and hours of an appearance. But President Edwin Hyde bridled at one demand of Gloria Swanson. "We're not putting down a red carpet at Byrd Airport," he said.

Besides the celebrity visitors the store enjoyed, another celebrity emerged from its own training program. Perry Ellis joined the store after graduation from Virginia Commonwealth University and soon was appointed Junior Colony sportswear buyer. His immediate success led to an affiliation with John Meyer, a vendor. From there Ellis moved

Fashion coordinator and Aldo Ray, a co-star of *Miss Sadie Thompson*. *Carol Bryson Private Collection.*

The Perry Ellis design influence lives on. *Collection of Perry Ellis Menswear Co.*

to New York, where he began designing scarves and, later, fashions, menswear and even home furnishings. He earned many fashion awards. Although he died in the early 1970s, his name continues as a significant influence.

One of M&R's most notable employees was Louise Orr, reputed to be "the top salesperson in the world" for Charles of the Ritz products. She once took a $300 order over the phone. She kept a card file of twenty-five thousand clients. The president of the Ritz company sent Mrs. Orr a letter of tribute before he sold the firm, and all of the Ritz face powder was sent to her so she could continue her custom blending in the

Louise Orr knew a thing or two about makeup. *Courtesy* Richmond Times-Dispatch.

Sara Sue traveled the world for hat design ideas.

"Designed for You by Sara Sue."

months before Miller & Rhoads closed. When Miller and Rhoads folded, she moved to Thalhimers, then to Hecht's at Regency Mall and to Dillard's at Willow Lawn. She retired at age ninety. As for her years at M&R, she said, "It was easy; I loved it." On her forty-fifth anniversary with M&R, the company gave her a party at the Country Club of Virginia, attended by executives of Charles at the Ritz. Her family was whisked to the party by limousine.[36] Sixteen years earlier, Charles of the Ritz had sent her off to London and Paris, where she gave an address and visited stores. Mrs. Orr had quite an influence on customers. Sometimes she persuaded them to buy cosmetics instead of clothes. "Even with old clothes, you can look beautiful, and, after all, you have only one face," she said."It's an investment to take care of it."[37]

Custom milliner Sara Sue was an institution within an institution. She was with the store for forty-two years and was important enough for the *MirroR* to devote an entire page to how her hats were composed. Waxing rhapsodic, the writer said that one particular season's hats had "colors borrowed from the stained glass windows of faraway Spain, Italy and the cathedrals of Paris—deep, glowing purples and greens, wines and blues." After attending showings in New York, Sara Sue was said to pick a theme and then visit "merchandising houses that cater entirely to custom shops…As she shops the houses, selecting each piece of material and trimming, models begin to form in her mind's eye for the customers she designs for year after year, and with whose wishes she is thoroughly familiar."

The entire process was described in detail, concluding: "When the final blocking has been done, the last bit of trimming tacked on, and the label, 'Designed for You By Sara Sue,' sewn in, our custom hat shop has completed another original creation which will be worn proudly by the customer—for she knows this hat has been designed exclusively for her…to emphasize her loveliness, individual style and love for all things that are beautiful."

Sara Sue kept a pincushion in her dress, and when she kept sticking pins in it, an observer worried that she'd hurt herself. She replied, "I had that one removed and use it for a pincushion. It doesn't hurt a bit."[38] The store paid for Sara Sue to visit Europe for inspiration, but when she asked to go to the Far East, General Manager Alfred Thompson nixed the idea and sent her two tickets to the musical *Kismet* instead.

CHAPTER 8

"WHERE CHRISTMAS IS A LEGEND"

The Thanksgiving-to-Christmas period is any department store's busiest season, but Christmas at Miller & Rhoads was more than just intense shopping. Display windows drew national attention; new shops opened just for the season; and Santa Claus did a lot more than listen to children on his knee recite their Christmas wish lists.

Of course, the store's interior was bedecked for the season from top to bottom. Since decorations had to be complete by Thanksgiving, it was necessary to begin work in early November. Even though the display staff began with holiday departments, such as Toys, Trim-a-Tree and Greeting Cards, other areas joined the red-and-green motif in mid-November. Invariably, some customers complained that "decorations are up too early."

Another store custom was sending special Christmas cards designed by Elmo Jones. Each year the theme was "Christmas Eve at [some historic house]." After the most prominent ones had been used, it was decided to use Elmington, the Gloucester County home of Webster Rhoads Jr.

During the season in the 1940s and '50s, "Felix the Clown" (Felix Adler) left the Ringling Bros. and Barnum & Bailey Circus and took up a station at Miller & Rhoads. He was replaced later by "Bruce the Spruce," a talking tree. Felix the Clown had a baby piglet, which he let impressionable children feed with a bottle. Diane Mugford said her mother would gladly leave her with the clown near the stockings on the main floor before meeting her under the clock and taking her to the Tea Room. Miss Mugford's maiden aunt lived with her and her mother and worked in Foundations at M&R. Nobody paid much attention to the little girl who peeked through "the crack of the pink curtains while Aunt Tee [Ethel Stone] would shove volumes of fat into these tight girdles while the unknown lady pulled mightily from the top. I was horrified. Many times there was a lot of naked lady extruding from the top and bottom of the device. As a teen-ager she fitted me with a 'merry widow' for the freshman-sophomore dance at Collegiate [School]. I could breathe, but eating and sitting were out!"[39]

For more than half a century, Addison Lewis was in charge of M&R's display windows, among which were the Madonna and Nativity windows, mechanical windows attuned to children and an elaborate electric train window. Lewis had a staff of thirty-four, including carpenters, artists and copywriters to prepare the store's fifty-five windows. He produced mannequins with natural-colored bodies and constructed of material that didn't melt with the heat. His motto was, "Don't sell me things; sell me romance and

Christmastime on the first floor.

Webster Rhoads Jr.'s home was a Christmas card setting. *Milton Burke Private Collection.*

Welcome, Felix, to Christmastime. *Carol Bryson Private Collection.*

glamour."[40] Lewis's windows were renowned far beyond the area from which Miller & Rhoads drew most of its shoppers, but no one was more critical than the passersby. One of them asked, "Why do you have a crying bride in the window?" Her comment was prompted by what appeared to be a tear on a mannequin. It was wax that had melted from a flower petal. Another worried about "a pregnant bride" that was the result of a swirl of material on a dress that made the bride appear pregnant.[41]

Catering to special groups of customers, Miller & Rhoads opened its Fawn Shoppe and Stag Shop during the Christmas season. The former was for children. Philip W. Klaus Sr. recalled how in the 1970s his grandchildren "went in alone and Santa's helper assisted them in making their selections. For three years in a row, I received soap on a rope."[42] Frances Crouch LaVecchia still has "the small, heart-shaped jewelry box…with the red felt lining" that her daughter bought for a dollar or two "with the help of sales clerks" in the Fawn Shop more than forty years ago.[43]

The Stag Shop was carved out of the men's department but was restricted to male shoppers. A female reporter for the *Richmond News Leader* recalled going to the Stag Shop to check on how it was doing. "All the little girls were fluttering around," the woman said, and there sat the governor, "with a big fat smile on his big fat face," enjoying himself immensely.[44] Spurred on by Christmas spirit, Governor William M. Tuck had proceeded to visit Santaland. Peggy Lee, who worked once in the Stag Shop, recalled a "quite rotund" man who continued smoking a smelly cigar while shopping for a nightgown for—he said—his wife. When asked about her size, he said, "About your size." The clerks were dubious about who the real recipient was.[45]

Madonna window, one of Addison Lewis's most notable.

Nativity window, another Addison Lewis production.

Above: Simple Simon window.

Right: A bag for every occasion: Fawn Shoppe at Christmas. *Milton Burke Private Collection.*

Governor Tuck visits Santa and the Snow Queen. *Colonial Studio Collection at Valentine Richmond History Center.*

With the success of the Stag Shop in Richmond, M&R decided to open one in Roanoke. It provided drinks in the Tea Room and put leopard-skin lingerie on display. The male shoppers thought that was fine, but women thought it was too much and returned it to the store.[46]

Miller & Rhoads was special to different customers for different reasons, but it was special to everyone for its clock, its tearoom and its Santa Claus. Indeed, its Santa was identified as the "real Santa Claus" by three generations of people from Virginia and beyond. From 1936 until the store closed, up to seventy thousand people a year visited Miller & Rhoads's Santa.[47] In 1951, the *Saturday Evening Post* carried an article on him, "The World's Highest Paid Santa Claus," by Clifford Dowdey, the Richmond-based author and historian. For $1,000 a week,[48] Santa camped out during the Christmas season in the Old Dominion Room on M&R's seventh floor. Children, many of them attired in their finest clothes, waited with parents for hours to visit Santa. He didn't see anyone until 9:30 a.m., but sometimes lines began forming two hours earlier.

When Santa was ready for a child, the youngster would wait for an instant with the Snow Queen, who would ask his name and relay it by a hidden microphone to Santa, who then beckoned and welcomed by name the astounded youngster. He was perched on Santa's knee long enough to recite his Christmas wish list as a store camera recorded the scene. Eager parents snapped up the pictures.

Donna Deekens became a Snow Queen while still an undergraduate at the University of Richmond and continued until the closing of the store. After college, when she came home from her job in Washington, she was a Snow Queen on weekends. Back in Richmond and working for the Valentine Museum, she took a week of vacation and, again, became a Snow Queen. She kept her original dress and wore it, until recently, as a Snow Queen for her Teapots, Treats and Traditions business.[49]

In her long reign as a Snow Queen, Ms. Deekens had moments of frustration, amusement and inspiration. "Little Johnny," about five years old, started out frustrating her because he was determined not to give her his name. After she and Santa waited longer than usual, he grudgingly told the Snow Queen who he was and immediately was dispatched to Santa, who, of course, called him by name. His mother told Johnny later how wonderful it was that Santa knew his name. Johnny replied, "But that damn dumb fairy didn't."

More rewarding was the visit near closing time one night from a poorly dressed black child, about twelve, who showed up alone. He told Santa what he wanted for Christmas was a drum set. Santa said he'd do what he could, but that was "a pretty big order." Ms. Deekens noted at the time a well-dressed man among the few adults remaining in the room who seemed quite interested in the little black boy. Later she learned that a "real drum set" had been delivered to the child's home, courtesy of that unknown man in the back of the room.

Carol Schlichtherle relished being a Snow Queen in the early 1970s. Heading up on an elevator to her job one day, she heard two boys "plotting to fool Santa Claus" by giving him false names and challenging him to identify them correctly. She learned the real names of "Sam" and "Jack" and told them to Santa by microphone. They were bowled over. "You could have had them for a nickel," she said. Through family connections, she knew various adults coming to Santaland and occasionally had Santa point out their peccadilloes. It was particularly embarrassing to one married man who was known to be playing around. Mrs. Schlichtherle said some adults stationed themselves on the front row and tried unsuccessfully to figure out how Santa learned what he knew.[50]

The first Santa was a man named Green, who came from a rural area and was sent to the beauty parlor to get cleaned up before his initial appearance. "There was everything but a dead mouse" in his unruly hair and beard, said Milton Burke, a longtime employee.[51] The next Santa, probably the most famous, was William Strother, a former Hollywood stuntman, who used a Max Factor custom-made wig, beard and makeup. "That wonderful Santa Claus thought he *was* Santa Claus," said John Marchant, retired M&R president.[52] Strother had built a reputation as the Human Fly, who would scale buildings all over the country. Webster Rhoads Jr. nixed the idea of Strother crawling down the side of Miller & Rhoads. "You may be the Human Spider," he is reported to have said, "but I'm not going to let you kill Santa Claus." Chris Rhoads, Webster Jr.'s son, said his father knew he'd made the right decision when Strother fell off a ladder the first day on the job as he was climbing into a device that would lower him onto the stage for his meeting with children.[53]

The waiting line for Santa was long, and sometimes it meant standing for hours. M&R executives made sure to adapt for special situations, and there were virtually no

"Original" Santa with Bill and Russell Jones. *Courtesy Frances Jones.*

complaints from those who were asked to hold back a bit longer. Such was the case with a four- to five-year-old boy who had been stricken with polio. He had never walked without braces, but he was determined to do just that. Santa and the Snow Queen were primed in case the child couldn't make it all the way to Santa's chair. He began walking and made it about a third of the way when he collapsed—into the arms of the waiting Santa. "There was not a dry eye in the room," said Robert Hardy, a vice-president.[54]

When Santa needed a lunch break, he went to the Tea Room, where he often saw the same children who had been on his lap earlier. After he mentioned that his cake was baked by Mrs. Claus, someone told him there was no Mrs. Santa Claus, so he switched the cake's origin to "Rudolph," Burke recalled.

Organist Eddie Weaver, who was stationed near Santa in the Tea Room, sometimes learned from a parent that a child was on the verge of becoming a nonbeliever in Santa Claus. Weaver would pass the child's name to Santa, who would call the child by name and say, "Thanks for coming to see me." "That was good for another year of believing," said Jody Weaver, Eddie's daughter.[55]

Donna Deekens thought Weaver was "the consummate entertainer—a true professional and extremely talented, but never pretentious." She ate lunch with him often in the Tea Room and even sang with him on occasion. With a change in ownership of the store in

The crowd is ready for a visit to Santaland. *Courtesy* Richmond Times-Dispatch.

the late 1960s, she said, she was told that "Snow Queens don't sing." Weaver comforted her by saying, "There will always be another show," which she took as advice for life. On occasion, he'd bend the rules and let her sing with him anyway. "What were they going to do—fire him?"

Miller & Rhoads's Santa didn't restrict his activities to the store. He lit the Christmas tree at the State Capitol and visited the children's ward at the Medical College of Virginia. From 1958 to 1971, he rode a "Santa Claus Train," which left Broad Street Station four times each Saturday, with one thousand children and five hundred parents aboard, and went to Ashland, sixteen miles away.[56]

Although there was officially only one Santa at a time, there were actually up to three because of the number of hours involved and the number of children to meet. One Santa was a Richmond actor, Hansford Rowe, who had attended the University of Richmond with one of the authors of this work. When his daughters were introduced, Santa asked, "How is Earle?"

"Daddy," they implored later, "do you really know Santa Claus?"

"Of course," he said. "We're old buddies."

Other Santas at M&R included Timothy L. Light, who filled the role from 1934 until his retirement because of poor health in 1939; Charlie Nuckols; Chuck Hood, who began in 1945 and continued until the store closed; and Dan Rowe, Hansford's younger brother, who began in 1966, stayed through Miller & Rhoads's closing and continued being Santa until the present. Now past eighty years old, Dan Rowe still delights in his role and relishes memories

The train window was a hit at Christmastime. *Courtesy Dementi Studios.*

of encounters with children across generations. He recalls one little girl in an ankle-length, obviously not new dress who showed up with her mother. When the child approached Santa, her mother pulled out a photograph of herself—in the same dress—with Santa.

About thirty-five years ago, a girl from Chincoteague presented Santa with a box when she came through the line at Miller & Rhoads. He left it closed until he got home, whereupon he opened it and found a quart of shucked oysters and more oysters still in the shell. Fast forward twenty-five years: a girl and a boy from Chincoteague came to see Santa. When he saw their mother standing by, he asked, "Mom, are you the…?" Before he could finish the question, she said, "Yes."

Rowe recalled a fiftieth wedding anniversary party at which a young couple, knowing he had been Santa, said they had talked about being photographed with Santa as five- or six-year-olds. They hadn't known each other at the time, but each produced a picture (they were numbered) from Santaland and found they were in line, virtually one behind the other, on the same day.[57] Santa received visitors regardless of age. One woman, perched on his knee, was asked what she wanted for Christmas. The immediate answer: "A husband."

Although Miller & Rhoads died in 1990, its Santa didn't. He moved across Sixth Street to Thalhimers and, when it folded, the legendary Santa moved to the Sixth Street Marketplace. As late as 2001, he made a Christmas appearance at the Westminster

Legendary Santa was a M&R trademark. *Milton Burke Private Collection.*

Canterbury retirement home. The *Richmond Times-Dispatch* carried an article on the visit, including a picture of ninety-four-year-old Catherine McNeil sitting on his knee. Now he's in the role at the Children's Museum in Richmond, where more than twenty-five thousand children visited in 2007.

The legendary Santa's low point occurred in 2004, when one of his "elves" working at the Richmond Convention Center stole his credit card. Santa declined to discuss the incident with *Style Weekly* newspaper. "It's an exciting time," said Santa. "I can't tell you anything else. All I know is the children. That's what Santaland is all about."

CHAPTER 9

BEYOND SALES

Miller & Rhoads's forays into public affairs really blossomed after World War II. Webster Rhoads Jr. and Edwin Hyde felt it was vitally important—for both sales and the store's reputation—to have the store participate in civic and charitable events in Richmond and the state as a whole. Hyde was named president in 1952, and for thirty years he encouraged his associates to become active in the community.

Some ten years earlier, the store had initiated its Book and Author Dinner, in which the Junior League was a partner. It was held in a packed Tea Room and featured several speakers each year. The dinner was the brainchild of Em Bowles Locker Alsop, a longtime Richmonder who had been impressed with the *New York Herald-Tribune*'s book luncheon and was determined that Richmond should put on something like it.

She said, "When I went to the Main Street Station to greet my first featured author, Betty Smith, whose *A Tree Grows in Brooklyn* topped all best-seller lists and was already considered an American classic, she asked at once, 'Where is Miss Locker?' When I said I was Miss Locker, she gave me an icy look and snapped, 'If I had known you were so young, I never would have come.'" But when Miss Smith and Miss Locker repaired to the John Marshall Hotel, where the author learned that Dr. Douglas Southall Freeman was to be host for the dinner, she decided things were not so bad after all. "She collapsed in the nearest chair, fanning herself vigorously as if in a dire faint," said Miss Locker. "Then she sighed deeply, stood up and declared, 'Now I know that I must be famous.'"

When Dr. Freeman agreed to be host for the event, he said, "My dear child, are you aware that you could be inaugurating a great Richmond tradition?" The event was such a success that Webster Rhoads telephoned with congratulations. The speakers the next year were Cornelia Otis Skinner and Emily Kimbrough, "whose *Our Hearts Were Young and Gay* was so popular that Peggy O'Neill and her assistant, Emma Craddock, said it was hard to keep [it] in stock," said Miss Locker.

When Miss Locker was chairman of the 1951 Book and Author Dinner, she suggested that there be a pre-dinner reception at the Valentine Museum for the authors. "I had learned as a volunteer at the museum that in the previous century, Dickens, Thackery, Washington Irving had been among those who strolled the boxwood paths, heard the fountain's falling waters, singing birds and swaying branches as guests…Since Robert Frost, the poet, was the featured author of my 1951 chairmanship, he was appropriately the first to stroll the same garden in their memory." That same year she persuaded a

M&R President Webster Rhoads Jr. and his successor, Edwin Hyde. *John West Private Collection.*

Junior League member to give "a post-dinner gala for the authors to unwind in pleasant circumstances with admirers." Both events became traditions.

Tickets were always hard to come by for several reasons, not the least of which was the reception at which ticket holders could mingle with speakers. They included Samuel Eliot Morison, Bennett Cerf, Bruce Catton, Cleveland Amory, Helen Hayes, Philip Wylie, Art Linkletter and Catherine Drinker Bowen. In 1960, two of the five speakers were that year's Pulitzer Prize winners. Over the years there were more than three hundred speakers.

The master of ceremonies for many years was Edward Weeks, editor of the *Atlantic Monthly*; he was followed by Peter Davison, Weeks's successor. They were followed by Paul Duke, moderator of Public Television's *Washington Week in Review*. With the aid of the Richmond Retail Merchants Association, the Junior League continued to sponsor the dinner after the demise of Miller & Rhoads. Mrs. Alsop was asked to help get a prominent speaker. She got in touch with her friend of half a century, Helen Hayes, the "queen of the American theater" but then ninety-one years old, and pleaded with her to come to Richmond. Miss Hayes demurred but, when assured by Mrs. Alsop that she would be picked up by limousine and flown to Richmond on a corporate jet, she accepted. The ticket and book sales set records, and Miss Hayes stayed signing books after the dinner until 2:00 a.m.[58]

Art Linkletter spoke at the Book and Author Dinner. *Collection of Junior League of Richmond.*

The Miller & Rhoads staff member most involved in the Book and Author Dinner was Emma Craddock, buyer and manager of the book department, who spent thirty-eight years with the store. She was involved with 113 authors at the dinners over the years. Miller & Rhoads was unusual in having its book department on the first floor, and Mrs. Craddock was unusual in how well she knew her customers and what books they liked to read. Not every bestseller nationally was a bestseller in Richmond. She also was amused by eccentricities she encountered. A story in the *Richmond Times-Dispatch* explained: "Once a woman brought in a piece of string to match with a length of books for a shelf. Another time Mrs. Craddock sold bedside books to match a piece of damask. And she recalls the customer who asked for an 'under the bridge' dictionary and the Sunday school teacher who stole 23 Bibles for his class over a period of time."[59]

Longtime friends Helen Hayes and Em Bowles Alsop. *Em Bowles Locker Alsop Private Collection.*

Blanche Satterfield and Emma Z. Brown directed the Women's Forum. *Emma Brown Private Collection.*

The Virginia Women's Forum was directed by one of Richmond's most beloved women—Blanche Satterfield. She was the widow of David E. Satterfield Jr., who had represented the Richmond area in Congress, and the mother of David E. Satterfield III, who had served city council, the Virginia General Assembly and Congress. Mrs. Satterfield was followed by Emma Z. Brown. A statement from M&R on the twentieth anniversary of the forum stated, "Your Forum Committees are interested, as always, in woman's place in a changing world; and they are confident that the best place is held and the best service is rendered by the informed woman."

Those women in Richmond were informed by such luminaries as Averill Harriman, adviser to presidents; Louis B. Wright, director of the Folger Shakespeare Library; Dean Rusk, president of the Rockefeller Foundation and later secretary of state; and Lewis Strauss, chairman of the Atomic Energy Commission.

Blanche Satterfield also helped arrange for a major Miller & Rhoads contribution to the Virginia Museum of Fine Arts. Webster Rhoads Jr. wanted to spread the word statewide about M&R, and Mrs. Satterfield had a close friend in the museum's business office, Muriel Christiansen. Together they worked with the Virginia Federation of Women's Clubs to promote the idea of a traveling art exhibition. The result was a custom-made traveling art exhibition. Artmobile I, donated by Miller & Rhoads, opened in Fredericksburg in 1953. Leslie Cheek, director of the museum, designed the vehicle. What the museum called America's first "gallery on wheels" caught on, and Artmobiles II, III and IV went on the road, thanks to gifts from the Old Dominion Foundation, the Carnegie Corporation, E. Claiborne Robins Jr. and—again—Miller & Rhoads.

Artmobile was first given by Miller & Rhoads. *Courtesy Virginia Museum of Fine Arts.*

Tobacco Festival float.

The Jamestown 350th anniversary merited a window.

Lewis James, a lecturer aboard the Artmobile for five or six years, said he learned the state of Virginia well—heading toward Appalachia in the fall, then back toward Richmond and later in the spring off toward the Eastern Shore. He recalled having an Andy Warhol picture of Marilyn Monroe in the exhibit and hearing viewers exclaim, "Look, it's Madonna."[60]

Miller & Rhoads's interest in public affairs didn't stop with cultural activities; it also involved politics. At a meeting of the National Industrial Conference Board in New York, President Edwin Hyde explained how he and other business leaders had formed Richmond Forward in 1963 and promoted candidates for city council the next year. Six of them filled seats on the nine-member council. The man responsible for the store's political activities was Thomas P. Bryan Jr., a vice-president and former mayor.[61]

The store also participated in such civic events as the Tobacco Festival and the Jamestown 350th anniversary celebration.

CHAPTER 10
THE TEA ROOM

Nothing epitomized the charm of Miller & Rhoads more than its Tea Room. Richmond matrons in hats and white gloves, after hearing the mellifluous voice of Simon Vaughan intone, "Tea Room, please," would board the special elevator to the fifth floor. For years they were greeted by a string trio or string quartet. For more than forty years afterward, the music came from the piano and organ of Eddie Weaver, who also was the organist at Loew's Theater at Sixth and Grace Streets.

"He ran back and forth for a long time," said his daughter, Jody, who occasionally substituted for her father on the rare days he was sick. Early in the morning his keyboard melodies would be piped through the store to "wake up the clerks," she said.[62] A former commentator for the fashion shows said Weaver had genuine liking for each model and chose his songs accordingly. When a junior model appeared, he would crank out, "Five-foot-two, eyes of blue..." And he wasn't above teasing his favorite matron model with, "The old gray mare..."

There was a variety of special fashion shows. Autumn Elegance was sponsored by female volunteers at the Virginia Home. Men About Town was put on by the women's auxiliary of the Medical College of Virginia with prominent local men as models. Jack and Jill, a black charity, held an event each spring. In addition, the store featured Candlelight Teas and the biannual Sara Sue shows. M&R fashion shows were traditions of several women's clubs, some using children as models.

Miller & Rhoads had a tearoom in 1919, but *the* Tea Room was established in 1924 and was divided into an Italian Room, an English Room and a Colonial Room. Six years later they were combined into one room decorated in "American Conventional."

Shoppers, of course, ate in the Tea Room, but everyone who ate there wasn't necessarily a shopper. Jody Weaver said that a group of businessmen had a table reserved five days a week and never had to wait in line. They were so established that their spot was named the Table Near the Organ, and there were letters addressed to them at TNTO c/o Miller & Rhoads. After the mid-1950s, businessmen were there in the "stag corner" off to one side, where women were not admitted until the early 1970s. Mothers with children in tow filled many of the five hundred seats in what was Richmond's largest restaurant. The scenery was attractive, especially since it included chic models showing off the latest fashions to women at lunch. The menu changed daily, and sometimes it was a race against the clock to get menus to the Tea Room by 11:00 a.m., a half hour before it opened.

Eddie Weaver and his daughter Jody perform in the Tea Room. *Courtesy Dementi Studios.*

Sue Ferrell and Tea Room shoppers.

Right: "Men About Town" fashion show in the Tea Room. *Courtesy Dementi Studios.*

Below: Young models Cabell Clarke and Kent Hudgens. *Carol Bryson Private Collection.*

Tea Room foyer, circa 1924. *John West Private Collection.*

For the Book and Author Dinner, banquet tables replaced the usual tables so that eight hundred people could be accommodated. Employees from many departments donned banquet gear to help out and remained until the early morning hours to reset the room for the next day's luncheon crowd.

Virginia Randall said she spent so much time waiting in line for a seat in the Tea Room that when Miller & Rhoads closed, she bought the "tables for 5 or more" sign. "It is now over my family room door that leads to the kitchen," she said.[63] John Marchant said the Tea Room just broke even; the idea was not to make money. Perhaps one reason was the

The Tea Room looked like this around 1935.

prices. In the early days, there was a fifty-cent lunch (baked apple, stuffed country sausage and butterbeans or cod fish cakes, egg sauce, creamed potato and pickled beets), a sixty-five-cent lunch, a seventy-five-cent lunch and even a one-dollar lunch (clam chowder, fruit cocktail, broiled tenderloin steak maitre d'hotel or chicken shortcake, giblet sauce, sweet potato croquettes, spinach au gratin, lettuce and tomato salad, ginger or vanilla ice cream, butterscotch sauce or chocolate cream roll). Hot rolls and tea, coffee or milk came with all the lunches.

Among Tea Room specialties were chocolate silk pie and, for a time, the Missouri Club, a sandwich developed by the store and not aimed at calorie counters. Between the two slices of bread were turkey and ham, and all was covered with melted cheese. The chocolate silk pie recipe was heavily laden and its recipe was a secret for years (see recipes at end of book).

Some former customers, describing their relationship with the store, sound as if these were almost religious experiences. Betty Bowe Timberlake of Morristown, Tennessee, said she went from baby clothes to school clothes to party dresses in the Girls' Department, and then to a new department—Preteen.

Miss Hannah told me that there were to be Preteen Fashion Shows and that a Miss Brayton was coordinating the runway models, who would be chosen soon. Girls are very brave at age 12, so I marched through the back corridors and offices behind the retail floors

Choose your lunch in 1924 in this setting.

until I found Miss Brayton's office, to tell her I wanted to be a model. I was chosen, and that was my first time with a paycheck!

Mother was pleased, too, and got me to all the rehearsals and shows, and enjoyed the whole scene, waiting for the cue, sashaying...down the runway, turning as the fashion narrator described the outfit, and smiling back to the always lively Eddie Weaver at the organ.[64]

The Tea Room stayed open to the public through January 12, 1990, although the store closed to shoppers six days earlier. In its last week, the Tea Room was packed with women, many in Sara Sue hats recalling the good old days. "She was the dowager queen of Miller & Rhoads," said one woman of Sara Sue. "She could do anything she wanted."[65]

Anne Pole Griffith, who modeled from 1963 to 1980, said, "The only thing I ever wanted to be was a Miller & Rhoads model." Nancy Pace Newton, who modeled for six years before teaching at the Collegiate School in 1967, said, "I'd come back one Saturday each Christmas season to model with Santa Claus."[66]

CHAPTER II

Employee Loyalty and Customer Service

Mary Easterly said that as a fourteen-year-old, "It was a big deal to go downtown, so I dressed up." Decked out in skirt, sweater, saddle shoes and white socks, hat and gloves—plus pearls—she rode a bus. At M&R, the elevator operator "would thrust his arm out as if holding the elevator for the Queen of England, wait until the elevator was filled with eager shoppers and then click his clicker two times for the doors to close." The elevator operators, Mrs. Easterly found, were "well-trained, respectable men who made the store elegant and less chaotic during the busy seasons."[67]

The store may be long closed, but there is still a tug that keeps former employees together for reunions. Some are nostalgic enough to have saved seemingly mundane mementos. Florence Jones Tignor, who worked in the better dresses department at the Willow Lawn Branch, said management told employees to "take whatever you want in the way of signs" when the store closed. She still has in her basement a sign of about sixteen by twenty inches of a Santa Claus sale.[68]

Jane Clough, who worked in sales at Willow Lawn for some twenty years, also wrote and directed plays performed by employees for employees in connection with sales at M&R. She was so good at it that the Willow Lawn Merchants Association asked her to write a play in which other stores could participate. It was presented in the S&W cafeteria in the same building with Miller & Rhoads.[69]

James Poole, who during World War II pushed carts of merchandise through the downtown store, is the son of Thelma Gordon Poole, who as a clerk in the business office received payments from customers around the world. The son is a philatelist and still has a collection of stamps dating back to 1955 that his mother received from M&R customers in South Africa, Italy, Cuba, France, Ecuador and the Philippines.[70]

At times, the attempts at exchange were comical. Dorman Hartley, vice-president of operations as late as 1980, said people often brought back Christmas purchases they had made across the street at Thalhimers. At least one customer tried returning half of a Smithfield ham. Another former executive said that "after New Year's, you always got some glasses with lipstick on them" for return.[71]

Sometimes looking out for a customer meant going beyond the confines of the store. One delivery truck was spotted at an ABC store. When questioned about it, the driver said he was buying whiskey for a Mrs. So and So, who lived in Windsor Farms, and she paid him back when he delivered it.[72] For years, Miller & Rhoads had a twice-a-day

Home delivery in the store's early years.

delivery; if a customer placed an order before noon, it was delivered later that day. One delivery involved a single item: a container of kitty litter.

Looking out for customers also meant strange hours for some employees. After learning of one Christmas Eve crisis, Miller & Rhoads began keeping one employee on duty until 11:00 p.m. each December 24 to avert a repetition. The store also had one employee, known in-house as the "shroud coordinator," who was available after hours to work with grieving survivors who needed proper burial attire for their recently deceased family member.

Charlotte Weinberg recalled that she was headed from Farmville to Florida, via Richmond, to pick up a mink stole at Miller & Rhoads. The trouble was that the Monday she was to have stopped in Richmond the store was closed because of the death of Webster Rhoads Jr. She telephoned the store and was told by an operator, "Stay where you are; someone will meet you at Miller & Rhoads to pick up your stole." She did as was told and an employee unlocked the store and fetched the stole.[73]

As a child, Libby Ford of Richmond went downtown on the bus on Saturdays and met friends "under the clock at Miller & Rhoads" before going to lunch and a movie. Later she shopped at M&R, picked out her wedding patterns there, took her children to see Santa Claus there and, of course, ate in the Tea Room. She worked in the Wedding

Services Department for five years and found it "such a joy to have the young brides-to-be come in and be able to help them select their patterns and write their invitations." For Mrs. Ford, "The loss of Miller & Rhoads was one of the largest losses that Richmond has ever had. The camaraderie of all the employees was magnificent."[74]

One employee who epitomized Miller & Rhoads was Milton Burke, a policeman's son who finished McGuire University School one day in 1942, went to work at the store the next day and stayed until retirement forty-four years later. An artist, decorator, arranger and designer, Burke was indispensable to the store. He never had a full-time assistant, but he had innumerable helpers depending on the job. He never considered leaving. "My bosses were good," he said.[75]

If someone didn't know that Burke has been married to the same woman, Bertha, for many years and had children and grandchildren, he'd think Burke had married Miller & Rhoads. The house that has been his home all his life is a virtual Miller & Rhoads museum. Scarcely an inch of wall space in any downstairs room is not covered with M&R memorabilia. The same holds true for floor space, with virtual aisles between stacks. Burke must have a sample of every shopping bag the store ever used. He has five rolls of plastic clothing bags, on each of which are a thousand sections—every one with an M&R logo. His wife uses them for trash.

For Burke, retirement from Miller & Rhoads doesn't mean separation from Miller & Rhoads. One of his pastimes is taking his large collection of Sara Sue hats to shows for elderly women. Another is hanging pictures for people who move to retirement homes. If a client insists on measuring, he's amenable; otherwise, he sizes up a room, makes a thumbprint on a wall and hangs a picture. One woman asked his fee and he replied five dollars. She gave him twenty-five.

In the store's 100th anniversary year, many former employees put on paper their feelings about their association with the store. Among them was Raymond E. Bowler, who began at age fourteen as a six-dollar-a-week stock boy who needed a permit to go to work. He retired in 1970 after "a wonderful happy experience for 47 years." When Bowler's wife became ill, Webster Rhoads Sr. inquired constantly about her and recommended medicines for her malady. Later, when Bowler was looking for a house, he told the inquiring Rhoads that he'd found what he wanted. Rhoads sent a junior officer to check on the brick bungalow and make sure the real estate salesman held it for Bowler for two days. Whereupon, Rhoads's secretary gave Bowler money for the down payment, and the Bowlers moved in two weeks later.[76]

Rhoads's generosity also was recalled by John M. Powell, who worked in the "visual merchandise" department. The paymaster at M&R was approached by Rhoads, who said, "Mollie, I hear stories of your charity works, and I want to help out. Here is a check for $5,000 to use in your endeavors as you see fit. When the money is used up, I'll give you some more. No questions asked." That was the source of Powell's Easter outfit.[77]

An example of the store's recognition of good service by an employee was the "better selling dollar," a two-dollar bill.

Besides the sales staff, there were employees at different locations, offering—without charge—various services. The most visible was the "lady under the clock," of whom there were several, but Kitty Duke was the best known. She changed money for bus

One of many different shopping bags. *Milton Burke Private Collection.*

Kitty Duke, the "lady under the clock." *Courtesy* Richmond Times-Dispatch.

The store's gift for outstanding sales. *Milton Burke Private Collection.*

fares, provided bus schedules, sold stamps and stocked brochures about goings-on in Richmond.

There was a customer service balcony for resting and for leaving notes. One day Anne Grimsley checked the book on the balcony after enjoying a movie and found that her husband, Ed, had "gone to Washington." The balcony also had a Thomas Cook travel office.

Everyone who worked for Miller & Rhoads was expected to keep his area immaculate. In the spring there were cages of live canaries behind various counters, and even cosmetics clerks were obliged to clean their counters and be sure the cages were clean. One employee, Raymond Cumby, had nothing to do but change light bulbs and, if he had time, scrape chewing gum from beneath counters.

A job seeker, no matter his or her background, couldn't simply go through an interview and take a challenging job. Scottie Arnest thought, incorrectly, that her degree in merchandising from Carnegie Tech assured her of a good position. She went through the standard eight months of training—from the mail room to being a gofer in Webster Rhoads's office—before becoming an assistant buyer in cosmetics.[78]

CHAPTER 12

Expanding in More Ways Than One

In the early 1950s, Miller & Rhoads and Thalhimers agreed that neither would expand in Richmond until 1960; however, both announced additional stores—M&R in Virginia and Thalhimers in North Carolina.

Once Miller & Rhoads decided to expand, it did so with gusto. In 1955, it opened branches in Charlottesville, Roanoke and Lynchburg. When retailing was expanding in the suburbs, Virginia's most prestigious department store was concentrating on downtown areas. Eventually, all three stores (Lynchburg's was the former J.R. Millner) were supplemented with outlets in malls—Charlottesville's Barracks Road in 1965, Roanoke-Salem Plaza in 1961 and Lynchburg's Pittman Plaza in 1960. The Millner/Miller & Rhoads store is memorialized in the old 1850s courthouse downtown that traces Lynchburg's history.

When Miller & Rhoads took over Millner's, it found that customers had figuratively been running the store. Some accounts, often those of the most affluent customers, were six months or more overdue. There was a huge inventory—especially of silver and china, because twelve-piece place settings had been ordered but never purchased as gifts for weddings. Another problem was a huge number of items that had been delivered "on approval" and had not been returned and for which there was no record.

The new management understood that the takeover of Millner's was not appreciated in Lynchburg, and it had to tread easily in making changes. It finally began service charges for accounts long overdue. It instituted a check-off system for items that had been ordered and not returned. The store eliminated special orders for customers who did not accept the merchandise until it had remained in stock long enough to be marked down.

One of the store's top customers was Louise Wallace, who operated the "best little whorehouse in Lynchburg." She routinely ordered new lingerie for each new girl at her house and got it "on approval." Louise's was a favorite stopping-off place for young men at the University of Virginia and other nearby colleges after they had left their dates at a proper women's college. Sometimes the young men became enamored of one of Louise's girls and asked her to a college dance. That being the case, Louise ordered the same clothing that a proper college girl would wear: a Davidow suit and proper blouse and shoes. It was all boxed up in a new suitcase and sent to the girl. It took a bit of arm-twisting for Louise to accept an end to the "on approval" arrangement, but she finally did.[79]

Lynchburg downtown store.

Thomas L. Mitchell, who managed M&R stores in Charlottesville and Roanoke, found that the branches had an array of characters no less distinctive than those in Richmond, where he also was manager. Barracks Road in Charlottesville had its Margaret Harris, a force not unlike Louise Orr in Richmond. Miss Harris had been owner of the Town and Country Shop, and her customers were among the city's elite, Mitchell said. A customer had to have an appointment with Miss Harris, who had many "big ticket" sales, including one Russian sable coat for $25,000.

At the earlier downtown Charlottesville store, a favorite customer was Marian DuPont Scott, owner of Montpelier, the home of former President James Madison; she usually appeared at the store late every fall in riding attire to order Christmas gifts for her employees.

In the Tea Room in Roanoke, Miller & Rhoads had a master baker, Darnell Johnson, whose specialty was a double-crust lemon pie, different from anything offered in Richmond. She also was noted for her pound cake, bread pudding and strawberry shortcake. When M&R closed, the Hotel Roanoke hired her immediately.[80]

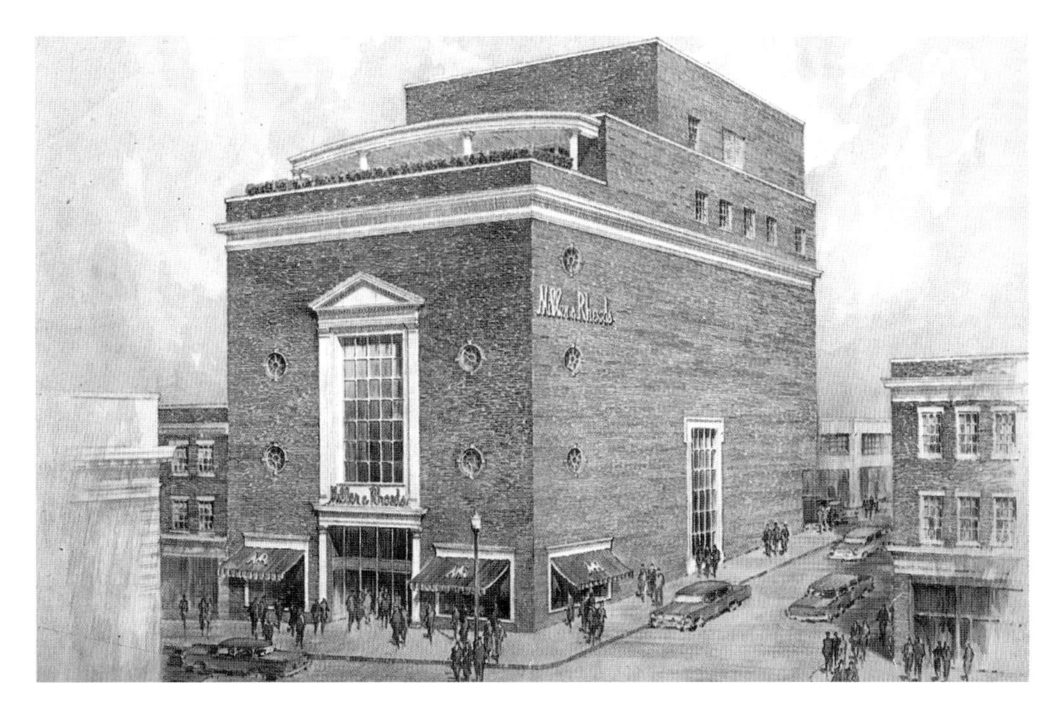

Charlottesville downtown store.

Roanoke downtown store.

Typical M&R suburban store.

The opening of the 112,000-square-foot store in Roanoke was accompanied by much hoopla. The dedication involved, in addition to M&R executives, the mayor of Roanoke, the chairman of the Roanoke County Board of supervisors, the president of the State Federation of Women's Clubs, the mayor and vice-mayor of nearby communities and a junior high school band. The *Roanoke World-News* newspaper devoted most of an eight-page news section that bordered on promotion to the opening.

It was major news in 1960 when Miller & Rhoads went to Willow Lawn, Richmond's premier shopping center. Webster Rhoads wanted the store to be taller than it was—two stories, later three—but Henrico County zoning restrictions precluded that.[81] During this period, Thalhimers built a Richmond West End store adjacent to its warehouse and new stores at Azalea Mall and Eastgate Mall.

M&R had planned to put a unit in Eastgate Mall, but in late December 1965 it announced it had changed its mind. President Edwin Hyde said that "since we originally expressed our intention of going into Eastgate, other new developments have occurred." He noted that the center was going to be considerably larger than first planned and "there appears to be a good bit of competition developing in the general area." What he did not say was that unknown to him, Thalhimers had decided to put a store there, and he felt there was not enough potential department store business in eastern Henrico for both.[82]

Miller & Rhoads then opened in Newport News in 1963, Norfolk in 1965 (buying Schwarz in the Southern Shopping Center), Southside Plaza in Richmond and Walnut Hill in Petersburg in 1965 and Pembroke Mall in Norfolk–Virginia Beach in 1966.

During the 1960s, Miller & Rhoads, Thalhimers and other traditional department stores expanded their customer base by extending a greater welcome to black shoppers. Sadly, this was not done voluntarily. The civil rights movement hit Miller & Rhoads in 1960. Although the store had black customers, it had not sought them out. Miller & Rhoads, and other downtown retail establishments like Thalhimers and the lesser lights such as Woolworth's, served meals. That meant they served meals to whites. They essentially were following customs of the Old South.

Young blacks, mostly students at Virginia Union University, were inspired by what they read of sit-ins at stores' lunch counters in cities south of Richmond. So on February 20, 1960, a group walked into Woolworth's, less than a block from Miller & Rhoads, sat down at the lunch counter and asked to be served. They were refused, so they moved to another store and, before the end of the day, they had staged sit-ins at five stores, including Thalhimers. All five closed their eating facilities, as did Sears, Roebuck, where no students had shown up. Police stood by but refrained from arresting anyone. Two days later, thirty-four Virginia Union students were arrested and charged with trespassing when they declined to leave Thalhimers after being refused service.

For six months, Miller & Rhoads and Thalhimers were picketed, as blacks and some whites urged them to desegregate. The mayor's biracial study committee recommended in August that all lunch counters be desegregated and that picketing be ended. Both department stores and the other stores serving meals followed the committee's recommendation—to a degree.

M&R released the following statement:

> *While it regrets that this move does not have the approval of all elements of the Negro population, it would like for it to be understood that what Miller & Rhoads is doing is in accord with decisions made and apparently accepted in all Southern cities which have accepted desegregation and which have both tea room and lunch counter facilities.*
>
> *These cities include Chattanooga, Nashville, Charlotte, Greensboro, Norfolk and Roanoke.*

But a black group, the Richmond Citizens Advisory Committee, urged continued picketing until all eating facilities stopped racial discrimination.

The tactics worked, or perhaps management had a change of heart. In any case, in January 1961, the Tea Room, as well as Thalhimers soup bar and the mezzanine at People's Broad Street store, admitted anyone who wanted to pay for his meal. Both department stores also opened their beauty salon doors and integrated their sales staffs.

The year 1960 also marked the 75th anniversary of the store's founding. The celebration was low-key and brief, unlike the 50th anniversary in 1935 and the 100th to come later. It was characterized by sales promotion and advertising, plus interior and window displays.

At that time the company said it was publicly committed "to strive for the finest in department store service" and installed a plaque to that effect under the clock downtown and at the pay bill desk in all branches.

Probably the most significant event of the decade was the decision in 1967 by M&R management and that of Julius Garfinckel & Co. to merge. This first of several mergers was a friendly one. Board Chairman Webster Rhoads Jr. told stockholders at a meeting June 15, "We believe in the advantages—to stockholders, employees and the public we serve—of community-oriented independent stores. The Garfinckel-Miller & Rhoads combination retains all of these advantages." Only 100 out of 303,941 common and preferred shares opposed the merger.[83]

14-C Richmond Times-Dispatch, Sunday, Jan. 31, 1960

Miller & Rhoads
THE Shopping Center
VIRGINIA'S FINEST DEPARTMENT STORES

Shop tomorrow 9:45 to 9;
other weekdays 9 to 5:30. Dial MI 8-3111.
See our double page spread in this paper
for exciting Anniversary News

"Miller & Rhoads
strives for the finest
in department store service, by way
of its merchandise, its personnel, its
customer facilities and good citizenship."

On this, the occasion of our Diamond Jubilee, we would like to share with you, our customers, the philosophy that has guided us throughout our 75 years of service to Virginia and surrounding states. It has been our goal—and will always be the path we shall follow toward that goal. It represents the guiding principle in our daily contact with you, our customers. In essence, it is more than words . . . it is a way!

It is our way of doing business; our way of handling personnel relations; our way of communicating our desires and objectives to our personnel and our customers. For 75 years this has been the Miller & Rhoads way. It is, we believe, the way in which Miller & Rhoads can best serve you.

This, then, is a reaffirmation of our goal . . . and a promise of

the path we shall follow toward it!

Entrance to the store from Grace Street.

Above: Window for the seventy-fifth anniversary.

Right: Christmas catalogue cover, seventy-fifth anniversary. *Dorman Hartley Private Collection.*

The store decided to stress its mission with a plaque.

The new corporate name was Garfinckel, Brooks Brothers, Miller & Rhoads. The new board of directors consisted of eight Garfinckel members and four Miller & Rhoads directors, including Lewis F. Powell Jr., later a justice of the United States Supreme Court. Rhoads was named chairman and Willard O. Bent was president and chief executive officer of Garfinckel, Brooks Brothers, Miller & Rhoads (GBM). When Rhoads suffered a heart attack and died two years later, Hyde was named chairman and CEO and John R. Marchant became president.

Besides Miller & Rhoads, the corporation consisted of Garfinckel's specialty stores in the District of Columbia, Brooks Brothers in upscale markets throughout the United States and de Pinna of New York and Palm Beach, which was closed shortly thereafter. Additional acquisitions include Hartzfeld's in Kansas City, Miller's department store in Tennessee and Ann Taylor nationwide.

The eclectic mix, while positive in profits and prestige, proved difficult to operate because of the divergent nature of department stores and specialty stores. Due to the

John R. Marchant, from elevator starter to president. *Courtesy* Richmond Times-Dispatch.

profitable nature of fashions and accessories, the GBM management decided that specialty stores were the way to go in expansion. The six specialty stores proved to be a major mistake, said Robert Hardy, an M&R vice-president.

Department store personnel were relatively unfamiliar with operating a specialty store. The result was that sales and profits were lower than expected. Later management opened eight larger full-line department stores in Richmond at Regency Mall and Chesterfield Town Center; in Tidewater at Lynnhaven and Greenbrier Malls; at Fashion Square in Charlottesville; at River Ridge in Lynchburg; at Newmarket North in Newport News; and at Valley View in Roanoke. The three western downtown stores were closed during that time. The problems of operating six specialty stores and eight new department stores helped contribute to the company's demise.

There were factors elsewhere—not the least of which was the steady movement of residents away from the cities and into the suburbs ever since the end of World War II. With that movement came warehouse clubs and discounters that paid little attention to customer service. In addition, "fair trade" laws, which let retailers decide what they thought prices should be, were repealed.

CHAPTER 13

MERGERS AND CLOSING YEARS

John Marchant retired in 1978 and Manny Rosenberg, the new president of GBM, appointed Charles C. Stanwood as president of Miller & Rhoads. Stanwood's previous department store experience had been at Jordan Marsh in Miami.

In a move to strengthen M&R management, Stanwood imported executives from his former company. A few were effective transplants, but a few were seen as the "goon squad" by their fellow M&R officers. Additional problems surfaced with Stanwood's temperament. Robert M. Hardy, vice-president, said Stanwood went to work at 4:00 a.m. one day, "threw mannequins around" and called a meeting of fashion executives.[84] Despite problems, Stanwood was personable and popular with the rank and file employees.

However, in January 1981, Rosenberg decided it was time for another change. Stanwood was elevated to chairman of M&R, and James F. Tornoe was appointed president. Tornoe had been an executive at Dayton Hudson in Minneapolis. Shortly after taking over he said, "I came for the long run. Nothing fancy. No flashes of brilliance." He acknowledged that Miller & Rhoads was having a difficult time but said, "I'd rather you characterize Miller & Rhoads as a company in transition."[85]

Tornoe's long run turned out to be rather short. He walked out of his office at 2:30 p.m. on May 29, five and a half months after taking the job. Stanwood, board chairman at that point, said, "He was not fired. We were very happy with him. I think he had a personal problem." Whatever the problem (Tornoe couldn't be reached that day for comment), he immediately joined J.L. Hudson Co. of Detroit, a Dayton-Hudson store, as executive vice-president.[86]

Tornoe wasn't the only executive to leave Miller & Rhoads. Within ninety days, the store also lost two vice-presidents, a personnel director and three divisional merchandise managers.[87] The next takeover involving Miller & Rhoads occurred fourteen years after the first, and it was anything but friendly. The board of what had become Garfinckel, Brooks Brothers, Miller & Rhoads voted August 13, 1981, to give top management a deal whereby its members would receive a lump sum package equal to three times their annual compensation if they left the company voluntarily within two years of a hostile takeover.

The next day, August 14, Allied Stores Corp. announced it was going after Garfinckel, whose chairman said he was "stunned." Allied and Garfinckel had been discussing

President Charles C. Stanwood.

whether Allied would buy Garfinckel's Miller & Rhoads division and a department store division in Tennessee, not whether Allied might go for the entire firm. Garfinckel's board opposed the move, but Allied got what it wanted in November.[88]

As soon as it gained control, Allied replaced Charles Stanwood, who had been president since 1978. For six months the store muddled along without anyone with the title of president. Then it filled the position with Robert J. Rieland, an experienced executive at Kaufmann's in Pittsburgh and Meier & Frank in Portland, Oregon. It also planned to stock more expensive merchandise and to spend $20 million improving existing stores.[89]

Although he was out as president, Stanwood was kept on at M&R as chairman for a year because Allied's president, Thomas M. Macioce, said he had to be given an office. "I don't know what he did," said Rieland. "I didn't talk with him at all." Rieland got rid of some executives who he thought weren't experienced merchandisers ("We had a good old boy network—like a fraternity") and brought in his own team;[90] but he was popular. Jerry Rutledge, secretary to three presidents, said Rieland was her favorite. He restored the "information desk lady" under the clock on the first floor, an M&R tradition that had been eliminated in the Tornoe days. Rieland mixed veterans with newcomers. "Unlike other Allied units which have been through this experience," he said, "we have not lost one soul. The carriage trade days are gone forever, but we want to bring back as many of the things that customers expect of Miller & Rhoads as we reasonably can."[91]

A major change to revitalize downtown occurred in 1984 with the start of the Sixth Street Marketplace. The Marketplace was a $27 million project involving not only Miller & Rhoads and Thalhimers, but also the Richmond banking community, the city administration, the federal government and the usual leaders in the arts community. The Marketplace bridge over Broad Street was supposed to be a symbol that linked blacks north of Broad and whites south of Broad. The "official" start of the construction on June 22, 1984, brought out the governor, both Virginia senators, the city manager, the mayor, the secretary of the U.S. Department of Housing and Urban Development and other assorted dignitaries.

Developer James W. Rouse, who had overseen similar revitalization projects in other cities, said, "Life in Richmond will be transformed." William B. Thalhimer Jr. said the project was "a guarantee for another 143 years" of his family's store, and M&R President Robert Rieland said, "We've always believed in downtown." Both stores contributed a million dollars toward the project, which provided a second-floor Sixth Street entrance to each after it was completed.

President Robert J. Rieland. *Courtesy* Commonwealth Magazine.

Sixth Street Marketplace, a dream for downtown. *Courtesy* Richmond Times-Dispatch.

Both department stores, of course, went at business full blast during the Marketplace construction. And before everything was in place, they announced they would be open on Sundays and at nights during the week.

The following year, Miller & Rhoads celebrated its 100th anniversary. No matter that it was now in a corporate situation that it didn't enjoy and no matter that downtown retailing was in a tailspin, Miller & Rhoads celebrated the anniversary with an exuberance that seemed to say things could hardly be better. Retro fashion shows were held in the Tea Room, with models who had appeared on runways as long ago as 1938. An exhibit of merchandise dated 100 years earlier was held in the Old Dominion Room. The public was invited (for twenty dollars a head) to a gala presentation at the Carpenter Center to feature the Richmond Symphony, Roberta Peters's singing and Peter Nero's piano playing. Performing arts groups would divide the proceeds.

Full-page advertisements heralded the store's anniversary. One, in *Women's Wear Daily*, was signed by

Retro models Willis Starbuck and Connie Augustine. Design by Anne Denny. *Courtesy Valentine Richmond History Center, Dementi Studios.*

Shopping bag marks 100th anniversary. *Milton Burke Private Collection.*

Richmond Times-Dispatch, Sun., July 28, 1985 J-7

enjoy
an evening with
Miss Roberta Peters
Mr. Peter Nero
Maestro Jacques Houtmann
conducting the Richmond Symphony

at the Carpenter Center
for the Performing Arts
Tuesday, October 15, 1985, 8 p.m.

**Tickets on sale beginning tomorrow
at the Carpenter Center**

All seats reserved, $20. To order, **call 782-3900**
Proceeds from all ticket sales will benefit: The Carpenter Center
for the Performing Arts, The Richmond Symphony,
The Virginia Opera Association/Richmond, The Richmond Ballet
presented by

Roberta Peters and Peter Nero performed for the 100th anniversary. *Robert Hardy Private Collection.*

President Robert Rieland and praised M&R's "partnerships with today's progressive manufacturers and suppliers." Back home, full-page ads in the Sunday *Richmond Times-Dispatch* touted a "birthday party" in the Tea Room, plus chances to win a round trip to London on the Concorde, a new Oldsmobile or a round trip on Singapore Airlines to the Far East. Governor Charles S. Robb's proclamation of October 17, 1985, as Miller & Rhoads Day merited another full-page M&R ad, and Thalhimers chimed in with a half-page ad saying that its across-the-street competitor had been "everything a good neighbor should be."

Robert Hardy and George Bryson as co-chairmen of the anniversary were designated to raise money from banks and manufacturers, a job they didn't like. "That's how Allied celebrated our one hundredth," said Bryson.

The gala at the Carpenter Center was just part of the celebration. It began with a cocktail party on the fourth floor of the department store, where furniture had been cleared. Invitees included eight hundred local dignitaries and fifty or so of M&R's top vendors. The second venue was the Tea Room, where the formally attired guests received Waterford crystal in addition to their dinners. The movable feast then proceeded to the Carpenter Center for musical entertainment. The evening ended with an ice cream party on the bridge of Sixth Street Marketplace.

A year after the big celebration, another unfriendly takeover occurred when Robert Campeau bought Allied Stores Corp. He was ruthless in cutting costs and determined to reduce the number of its stores from 684 to 274.[92] Most of the reduction came from his selling off specialty stores like Garfinckel's, Bonwit Teller and Brooks Brothers and department stores such as Miller & Rhoads and Jordan Marsh.

In June 1987, Miller & Rhoads was bought by Kevin Donohoe, a Philadelphia real estate developer. He held 85 percent of the stock, with the balance purchased by several Miller & Rhoads officers including Rieland, Marvin Lutzger, John Stokeley, Chris Zubov and Robert Hardy. The new owners announced plans to close the Chesterfield store and expand markets into Charleston, South Carolina, and other Southern cities. The move was on for more upscale goods, while some key budget lines were discontinued. This proved disastrous for profits and led to serious consequences.

Within the next year, Rieland and Lutzger resigned and Rieland moved across Sixth Street to become president of Thalhimers. Stokeley was chosen his successor for one year. He was a bright and capable executive but it was too late to save the ship. His principal role was to "turn out the lights."

The store went into bankruptcy in late 1989 and closed for business in January 1990.

CHAPTER 14
FAREWELL

The famous Miller & Rhoads clock had to be repaired occasionally. Once, when so many customers asked about its status, Milton Burke, the display wizard, put up signs on each side of the clock. They read:

Out for 50-year checkup
Hickory Dickory Dock; It's time to fix the clock
Hour spring has sprung
Good times will soon return.[93]

The clock now occupies a prominent space at the Valentine Museum, thanks to former employees of the store. In 1990, eight old-timers got together and sent letters to 1,248 of their ex-colleagues asking them to contribute to a fund to buy the clock, which had been installed at M&R when it expanded on Grace Street in 1924. A Philadelphia appraiser figured the clock was worth $15,000. At an auction, the Valentine won the clock with a bid of $12,000, all of which came from those former employees.[94] All of the store's furnishings were not auctioned off. Jack West, grandson of Webster Rhoads Sr., gave the chairs and table from the executive dining room to Randolph-Macon College.

The Santa Claus chair was to be auctioned off, too, so Vice-president Robert Hardy decided to make a real event of the sale. He accompanied Dan Rowe, dressed in Santa's true regalia, to the basement, where the auction was to take place. Each of the dozen or more prospective bidders had a chance to chat with Santa. When they learned that he treasured his chair and was going to try to keep it, all said they certainly would not bid against Santa. Hardy told Santa, "If someone goes against you, raise your hand." They set $1,500 as the maximum they would bid. When the auctioneer went into action, one man raised his hand immediately after Santa made a bid. Hardy was convinced the bidder was a shill for the auctioneer. In any case, Santa got his chair for $1,500 and took it with him when he moved across Sixth Street to Thalhimers.[95]

The last day of business was to be Saturday, January 19, 1990. Thomas L. Mitchell, last general manager of the downtown store, recalls it:

I was told by the then president, John Stokeley, on Thursday prior that that would be our last day to be open. I want you to know that I will never forget that day. The store was

Larry Walters dismantles the clock, an M&R icon.

There was sentimental attachment to Santa's chair. *Robert Hardy Private Collection.*

A different scene from earlier years. *Courtesy* Richmond Times-Dispatch.

> *visited by thousands of people to say their last good-byes. I knew from the turnout that the store was truly loved by Richmonders and the state of Virginia. Customers stood in long lines buying anything that would be a memento to keep. Nothing was on sale, but they still bought it.*
>
> *I do not remember the exact sales figures, but they were easily about six times what we normally would have sold on a Saturday. Two thousand people ate in our Tea Room, vs. a normal Saturday of about 100. Everyone and everybody came out to wish us farewell. I stood under the clock greeting people. The Senior Mrs. Ukrop related to me how she had been a waitress in our Tea Room in 1933. That day was one of the saddest days in my life and at the same time one of the happiest knowing how much the store was loved by the Richmond public.*[96]

Doris Daniel, who worked in the Boy Scouts division of the boys' department for fifteen years before departing in 1961, returned to the Tea Room the day it closed twenty-eight years later. When she found her former boss, Robert Hardy, "We met there and talked and cried," she said. Mrs. Daniel doubted that the store made much money from handling Scout uniforms, books and equipment, but she thought it was good public relations.[97]

On the last day of business, Miller & Rhoads had its equivalent of the Gettysburg Address, and its brevity even surpassed that of Abraham Lincoln. Vice-president Robert Hardy said simply,

Ladies and gentlemen, to our guests who may still be shopping and to our loyal associates, Miller & Rhoads is proud of its 104-year heritage, its people, and its contributions to our community.

It is with some sadness, but also with great pride that we now close our door tonight for our last day of regular business. It's now 5:30 p.m. Thank you for shopping with us, and you may now leave through the Fifth Street exit in the men's area.

Good evening and good bye.

Epilogue

Following the official closing, the store remained open for about three months with the liquidation of merchandise, furnishings and fixtures. After the furor of the "out-of-business" auction ended, the downtown store became a desolate place. The GE Acceptance Corp., which owned the building, hired Henry G. Coghill, a former sales executive of M&R, as its sole representative to handle the property and any customer service that might arise. Coghill reported that "it was a lonely job." In addition to physical maintenance, he was responsible for answering the telephone for customers who had not received word of the closing. In one instance, a customer sent in her expensive fur coat for storage. Despite several registered letters and a determined search to locate her, he was unsuccessful. Eventually, when she could not be found, the coat was given to charity.

Each year Coghill offered to resign, but GE implored him to stay because it believed that a sale of the property was imminent. The downtown property continued to deteriorate, and Coghill resigned after seven years because the City of Richmond would not even accept the building as a gift. Finally, interest was shown by ECI Investment Advisors, which chose Commonwealth Architects to investigate the feasibility of converting the building into condos or a hotel.

The person who probably has spent the most time in the old Miller & Rhoads building since its closing is Chad Clinger, who, as head of a team from Commonwealth Architects, explored the structure from top to subbasement in preparation for its conversion to a hotel/condo. The building was without electricity. Clinger found his task "eerie, but exciting nonetheless." At first he became disoriented, but "as time went on, I came to know the building very well." He said,

> *Generally, you could still see the old finishes, display shelves, etc., in the sales areas, so a rush of memories would come with almost every turn of the corner. I even documented the old Tea Room, with its now buckling floors and peeling paint, but I could still remember it during its finer times…*
>
> *The escalator was no longer in operation, so we climbed it as a means of access to the upper floors. There were a few items referencing the connection to Miller & Rhoads that we salvaged from the building, including some signage and customer account receipts, but I left most of that to the firm with whom I was employed. I had hoped to salvage one of the "fallout shelter" signs from the exterior of the building, but those had already been pilfered. Like the "fallout*

Construction for renovation, 2008. *Carolyn Moffatt, photographer.*

> *shelter" signs that once existed there were other references to the past that did still exist within the walls of the old store, including painted signage to a restroom door that stated "colored."*

During renovations outside on the street, concrete had been dumped in the basement loading area, and "it looked like a bombed-out war zone."

"In other areas," said Clinger, "the paint was peeling off in stalactite formations, tiles were loose and carpet moist from the lack of maintenance and infiltration of water. Pigeons had made their home in almost every perimeter space from the second floor up to the top. Luckily, I never saw a rat or mouse."

Clinger said there was not only a basement but also a sub-basement, beneath which was an artesian well. When Milller & Rhoads was operating, so was a sump pump, but now there were several feet of water in the subbasement. Clinger and a colleague donned boots, "navigating through the inch or so of residual mud to measure the space. Again, with only battery-powered lanterns to light our way."

In the empty building there was always a guard. One of them told Clinger that early one morning the fire department showed up, and he wondered why since he hadn't called. It turned out that a homeless person had found his way to the second floor, became panicky and yelled to someone on the street to help him find his way out.[98]

Fortunately, the architects decided that with vision, determination and about $100 million, the conversion was a go. The ECI Co. tackled the job in 2006.

The Hilton Garden Inn with 250 rooms will occupy seven floors of the western portion of the former M&R store. The Woolworth building has been demolished and replaced with a porte-cochere and underground space for parking 250 cars along with space in existing subbasements. Two atriums have been created to provide light to inside areas.

The Miller & Rhoads condominiums will have 132 units in the old store's eastern half, with the entire eighth floor as penthouses. Again, there will be the chance for sunbathing on the roof and for the first time swimming and fitness space inside.

Any chance of "customers" huddling under an M&R clock again?

APPENDIX

Tea Room Recipes

Miller & Rhoads's Chocolate Silk Pie

Crust:
½ cup each of butter and granulated sugar
2 cups graham cracker crumbs

Filling:
½ cup unsalted butter
¾ cup confectioner's sugar
1 ounce unsweetened baking chocolate, melted and cooled
pinch of salt
1 teaspoon vanilla extract
3 eggs

Garnish:
2 cups sweetened whipped cream
chocolate Jimmies or shaved semisweet chocolate

Begin crust by beating butter and granulated sugar with electric mixer until light and fluffy. Gradually mix in just enough crumbs to make a slightly crumbly paste. Press evenly into a chilled eight- or nine-inch pie plate. Bake in a preheated 350-degree oven for five minutes. Cool to room temperature.

Begin filling with an electric mixer by beating butter and confectioner's sugar until light and fluffy. Add melted chocolate with salt and vanilla. Add one egg and beat for no less than five minutes. Add second egg and beat no less than five minutes longer. Add third egg and beat no less than five minutes longer. Pour filling into prepared shell and refrigerate twenty-four hours.

Just before serving, decorate top with sweetened whipped cream and sprinkle with chocolate.

Missouri Club Sandwich (serves 8)

Mustard pickles:

1 pint sweet mixed pickles, drained
6 scant tablespoons sugar
¾ teaspoon cloves, ground
2 tablespoons prepared yellow mustard

Place drained pickles in bowl and sprinkle with sugar and cloves. Stir thoroughly. Stir in mustard until evenly coated. Cover and refrigerate overnight to allow sugar to dissolve. Stir again before serving. Makes 2 cups.

Basic club sandwich:

16 slices bread, toasted
8 slices turkey deli meat
8 slices ham (prefer Virginia ham)
8 (1-ounce) slices American cheese
8–16 slices tomato
mustard pickles
8 jumbo olives, stuffed
16 slices bacon, cooked crisp (optional)

Toast bread and build basic club sandwich with turkey, ham, cheese, tomatoes, pickles, olives and bacon.

White sauce:

8 tablespoons butter
8 tablespoons flour
4 cups milk
2 teaspoons salt
½ teaspoon white pepper
½ pound Colby cheese, grated

Melt butter in saucepan and slowly add flour to form a smooth paste. Add milk, salt and white pepper and bring to a boil over medium heat, stirring constantly. After the mixture begins to bubble and boil, continue cooking one more minute. Stir in grated cheese until melted. Remove from heat.

Prepare the sandwiches, mustard pickles, bacon and sauce in advance of serving. When ready to serve, pour white sauce over each club sandwich and place them under the oven broiler until the cheese sauce bubbles. Remove and serve sandwiches with olives, bacon and mustard pickles.

Notes

Chapter 1

1. Recollection of Kathleen Duke, 1985, at 100th anniversary get-together of retired employees.
2. Recollection of Robert Moran, 1985, at 100th anniversary.
3. "We're Going Places Together," company publication, 1947.
4. Recollection of Mary Coleman Hankins Wingfield, 1985, 100th anniversary.

Chapter 2

5. William S. Lacy Jr., "Miller & Rhoads, a Virginia Institution," *The Commonwealth, the Magazine of Virginia*, June 1958.
6. *Richmond, Virginia, and the New South* (Richmond: Geo. W. Engelhardt Co., circa 1888), 150–51.
7. Interview with her daughter, Mrs. Robert Seiler, May 26, 2008.
8. Interview with author, April 22, 2008.
9. Letter to author from Thomas L. Mitchell, May 28, 2008.
10. Webster Rhoads Jr. address to Newcomen Society in North America at Commonwealth Club, Richmond, 1960.
11. Recollection of Judy Bolling, 1985, 100th anniversary.
12. Recollection of Gladys Jett, 1985, 100th anniversary.
13. Author's correspondence with her grandson, Dr. Jerome D. Becker, June 3, 2008.
14. Rhoads's address to Newcomen.
15. Ibid.

Chapter 3

16. Letter to author, June 20, 2008.
17. Letter to author, May 27, 2008.
18. *House Beautiful*, "The Queen of Accessories," June 2008.

Chapter 4

19. Interview at his home, January 18, 2008.
20. Interview with author, June 16, 2008.

Chapter 5
21. Louise Lipscomb, "Memories of Miller & Rhoads," *Style Weekly.*
22. Interview at his home, January 18, 2008.
23. Interview with author, June 17, 2008.
24. Interview with Chris Rhoads, June 16, 2008.
25. Letter to author, June 16, 2008.
26. Interview with author, June 17, 2008.

Chapter 6
27. Lipscomb, "Memories."
28. Note to author, 2008.
29. Pat Pontius, "Miller & Rhoads: Birth, Life, and Death in a Community" (undergraduate paper at University of Virginia, 1999).
30. Letter to John West, February 6, 2008.
31. Pontius, "Miller & Rhoads."
32. Interview with author, June 16, 2008.
33. Letter to author, May 24, 2008.
34. Letter to author, May 27, 2008.
35. Recollection of Jane Straughan, 1985, 100th anniversary.

Chapter 7
36. Barbara M. Ingber, "Saleswoman Extraordinaire," *FiftyPlus* newspaper, October 2002.
37. Betty Pettinger, *Richmond Times-Dispatch*, October 2, 1982.
38. Interview with Milton Burke, April 22, 2008.

Chapter 8
39. Letter to author, June 10, 2008.
40. "We're Going Places Together," company publication, 1947.
41. Interview with Milton Burke, April 22, 2008.
42. "Miller & Rhoads eulogy," at final meeting at M&R of Richmond Rotary Club, January 16, 1990.
43. Letter to author, 2008.
44. Conversation with author, winter 2008.
45. Note to author, 2008.
46. Interview with John Marchant at his home, January 18, 2008.
47. Kristin Terbush Thrower, *Miller & Rhoads Legendary Santa Claus* (Richmond: Dietz Press, 2002), 123.
48. Letter to author, May 27, 2008.
49. Letter to author, May 29, 2008.
50. Interview with author, June 10, 2008.
51. Interview with author, April 22, 2008.
52. Interview at his home.
53. Interview with author, June 16, 2008.

54. Interview with author, June 18, 2008.
55. Interview with author, June 9, 2008.
56. Thrower, *Legendary Santa Claus*, 85–86.
57. Interview with author, June 4, 2008.

Chapter 9
58. Alsop letter to George Bryson, June 20, 2008.
59. Louise Ellyson, *Richmond Times-Dispatch*, April 30, 1968.
60. Interview with author, May 23, 2008.
61. *Richmond News Leader*, April 21, 1966.

Chapter 10
62. Interview with author, June 9, 2008.
63. Letter to author, May 31, 2008.
64. Letter to author, June 3, 2008.
65. Katherine Calos, *Richmond News Leader*, January 12, 1990.
66. Ibid.

Chapter 11
67. Unpublished memoir, 2008.
68. Recollection of Judy Bolling, 1985, 100th anniversary.
69. Letter to author, June 20, 2008.
70. Interview with author, May 28, 2008.
71. Meeting with former executives, February l, 2008.
72. Interview with John Marchant at his home, January 18, 2008.
73. Interview with author, June 5, 2008.
74. Letter to author, June 2, 2008.
75. Interview with author, April 22, 2008.
76. Recollection of Raymond Bowler, 1985, 100th anniversary.
77. Recollection of John M. Powell, 1985, 100th anniversary.
78. Interview with author, June 4, 2008.

Chapter 12
79. Interview with author, June 20, 2008.
80. Letter to author, June 16, 2008.
81. Interview with Chris Rhoads, June 16, 2008.
82. *Richmond News Leader*, December 23, 1965.
83. Tyler Whitley, *Richmond News Leader*, June 15, 1967.

Chapter 13
84. Suskind and Hardy meeting with authors, February 1, 2008.
85. John Dillon, *Richmond Times-Dispatch*, January 22, 1981.
86. Ibid., May 30, 1981.
87. Ibid., June 5, 1981.

88. Steve Row, *Richmond News Leader*, August 22, 1981.
89. Interview with author, May 30, 2008.
90. Telephone interview with author, May 20, 2008.
91. *Virginia Business* magazine, August 1987.
92. Isadore Barmash, *New York Times*, February 14, 1988.

Chapter 14
93. Recollection of Kathleen Duke, 1985, 100th anniversary.
94. *Richmond Times-Dispatch*, March 14, 1990.
95. Letter to author, May 28, 2008.
96. Letter to author, May 31, 2008.
97. Letter to author, June 9, 2008.

Epilogue
98. Letter to author, June 12, 2008.

About the Authors

Earle Dunford. *Carolyn Moffatt, photographer.*

Earle Dunford is an army veteran of World War II and a graduate of the University of Richmond. He joined the *Richmond Times-Dispatch* in 1952 and covered a variety of beats, including courts, local government, crime, education, business and labor. He became city editor in 1969 and held that post for almost twenty years until retirement. He was an adjunct instructor in journalism at the University of Richmond for a quarter-century and was Virginia correspondent for the former *National Observer*, a weekly Dow Jones newspaper. He is the author of *Richmond Times-Dispatch, the Story of a Newspaper*. He has two daughters and two grandchildren.

Following his graduation from Hampden-Sydney College, George Bryson joined Miller & Rhoads in 1950 and held early positions in personnel, customer service and buying. His store management experience included Roanoke, Lynchburg, Virginia Beach and downtown Richmond. He was vice-president of fashion and accessories and later executive vice-president of store management and operations. He "retired" in 1989 as vice-president for public relations. Then for sixteen years he enjoyed a career with the Virginia Museum of Fine Arts Foundation. He has five children and six grandchildren.

George Bryson. *Carolyn Moffatt, photographer.*